Instructor's Manual

for

Writing and Reporting News
A Coaching Method
Fourth Edition

Carole Rich
Hofstra University

THOMSON

WADSWORTH

Australia • Canada • Mexico • Singapore • Spain • United Kingdom • United States

Printed in the United States of America
1 2 3 4 5 6 7   05 04 03 02 01

Printer: Victor Graphics

0-534-56284-1

For more information about our products, contact us at:
Thomson Learning Academic Resource Center
1-800-423-0563

For permission to use material from this text, contact us by:
Phone: 1-800-730-2214
Fax: 1-800-731-2215
Web: http://www.thomsonrights.com

Asia
Thomson Learning
5 Shenton Way #01-01
UIC Building
Singapore 068808

Australia
Nelson Thomson Learning
102 Dodds Street
South Street
South Melbourne, Victoria 3205
Australia

Canada
Nelson Thomson Learning
1120 Birchmount Road
Toronto, Ontario M1K 5G4
Canada

Europe/Middle East/South Africa
Thomson Learning
High Holborn House
50/51 Bedford Row
London WC1R 4LR
United Kingdom

Latin America
Thomson Learning
Seneca, 53
Colonia Polanco
11560 Mexico D.F.
Mexico

Spain
Paraninfo Thomson Learning
Calle/Magallanes, 25
28015 Madrid, Spain

Contents

Introduction

1   *Write From the Start: A Coaching Method*   1

Teaching Suggestions   1
Textbook Exercises
1. Visual/verbal news story   2
2. Reaction story   3
3. Online focus exercise   4
4. Find the focus   4
5. Online quiz   4
Workbook Exercises
1-1. Crime story   4
1-2. Find the focus   5
1-3. Online focus: headlines and blurbs   5
1-4. Visual elements   6
1-5. Style quiz corrections   6

2   *Changing Concepts of News*   7

Teaching Suggestions   7
Textbook Exercises
1. Reading experiment   8
2. Journal   8
3. Graphics   8
4. Brainstorm online news ideas   9
5. Interactive quiz   9
6. Test your news judgment   9
Workbook Exercises
2-1. Online news qualities   9
2-2. Convergent media   9
2-3. Public (civic) journalism   10
2-4. Qualities of news   10
2-5. Hard-news and feature stories   10

3 *The Basic News Story* — 11

Teaching Suggestions — 11
Textbook Exercises
1. Basic news story #1 — 12
2. Quotes and attribution — 13
3. Enterprise — 13
4. Class reunion feature — 13
5. Online census story — 13
6. Online textbook quiz — 14
7. Basic news story #2 — 14
Workbook Exercises
3-1. Fire — 15
3-2. Program advance — 15
3-3. Online version — 16
3-4. Burglary — 16
3-5. Telephone bill — 17
3-6. Quotes — 17
3-7. Punctuating quotations — 18
3-8. Style quiz corrections — 19

4 *Grammar and Usage* — 20

Teaching Suggestions — 20
Textbook Exercises
1. Grammar A-K — 20
2. Grammar L-Y — 21
3. Edit a Story — 21
Workbook Exercises
4-1. Active vs. Passive Voice — 22
4-2. Action Verbs vs. Linking Verbs — 22
4-3. Dangling Modifiers — 23
4-4. It's, Its — 23
4-5. That, Which — 23
4-6. Who or Whom — 23
4-7. Run-on Sentences — 23
4-8. Subject-Verb Agreement — 24
4-9. General Usage — 24

5 *Curiosity and Story Ideas*   25

Teaching Suggestions   26
Textbook Exercises   27
(Self-explanatory; no separate discussion)
Workbook Exercises
5-1. Coaching exercise   27
5-2. Three ideas in 15 minutes   28
5-3. A-Z brainstorming   28
5-4. Localize national news   28
5-5. Special sections   28
5-6. Classified advertisements   29
5-7. Plan an online newspaper   29
5-8. Curiosity training   29
5-9. Descriptive writing from observation   29
5-10. Analogies   29

6 *Sources and Online Research*   30

Teaching Suggestions   30
Textbook Exercises
1. Cross directory   31
2. Databases   32
3. Reports   32
4. Record search   32
5. FOIA request   34
6. Enterprise story   34
7. Online scavenger hunt   34
Workbook Exercises
61-2. Self explanatory
6-3. Online sources   37

7 *Interviewing Techniques*   38

Teaching Suggestions
Textbook Exercises
1. Interview a reporter   39
2. Icebreakers   39
3. Note taking   40
4. Notes   40
5. Police office   40

6. Technical clarity   40
7. Graphics   41
8. Enterprise story   41
Workbook Exercises
7-1-3. Listening, interviewing, concentration   41
7-4. Coaching   41
7-5. Observing interviewing techniques   41
7-6. E-mail interview   42
7-7. Interview a news source   42
7-8. Beyond the 5 W's   42
7-9. Dissect a newspaper story   42

8 *The Writing Process*

8 *The Writing Process*   43
Teaching Suggestions
Textbook Exercises
1. Write a plan for organizing a story   44
2. Free-writing   44
3. Revision   44
4. FORK exercise   44
5. Web story   46
Workbook Exercises
8-1. FORK exercise   46
8-2. Revision to tighten and correct style   48
8-3. Style test   49

9 *Leads and Nut Graphs*

9 *Leads and Nut Graphs*   50
Teaching Suggestions   50
Textbook Exercises
1. Hard-news leads   51
2. Active/passive voice   52
3. Delayed identification   52
4. Updated lead   52
5. Impact leads   52
6. Attribution   52
7. Anecdotal focus-on-a-person lead   53
8. Specific to general   53
9. Descriptive lead   53
10. Narrative lead   53
11. Leads analysis   54
12. Web leads   54
Workbook Exercises
9-1. Hard-news (summary) leads   54

9-2. Delayed identification leads   55
9-3. Second-day leads   55
9-4. Impact leads   56
9-5. Attribution in leads   56
9-6. Soft leads   56
9-7. Summary and soft leads   58
9-8. Style quiz corrections   59

10 *Story Structure*

10 *Story Structure*   60

Teaching Suggestions   60
Textbook Exercises
1. Inverted pyramid   61
2. *The Wall Street Journal* formula   61
3. Hourglass exercise   63
4. List technique   63
5-6. Sections and Web story (self explanatory)
Workbook Exercises
10-1. Endings   64
10-2. Bright endings   64
10-3. Inverted pyramid   65
10-4. *The Wall Street Journal* formula   67
10-5. Hourglass exercise   68
10-6. List technique   69
10-7. Style test   70

11 *Storytelling and Feature Techniques*

11 *Storytelling and Feature Techniques*   71

Teaching Suggestions   71
Textbook Exercises
1. Scene   72
2. Analogies   72
3. Narrative writing   72
4. Web storytelling   73
5. Timed free writing   73
Workbook Exercises
11-1. Storytelling mindset exercises   73
11-2. Storytelling for a crime story   73
11-3. Storytelling news feature   75

12 *Public Relations Writing*   76

Teaching Suggestions   76
Textbook Exercises
1. Campus event press release   76
2. Devise a media kit   77
3. Write a news release   77
4. E-mail news release   77
5. Public service announcement   77
6. Promote a product   78
Workbook Exercises
12-1. Qualities of news releases   78
12-2. Gather information and write news releases   78
12-3. Rewrite a news release   79
12-4. News release   80
12-5. News feature release   81
12-6. Web news release   84
12-7. Product promotion - print and Web   85
12-8. Interviews for news release format   86
12-9. Design a media kit   86
12-10. Creative preview publicity planning   86

13 *Broadcast Writing*   88

Teaching Suggestions   88
Textbook Exercises
1. Broadcast brief   89
2. Louisville chase   89
3-5. Newscasts and teasers   90

Workbook Exercises
13-1. Church embezzler   90
13-2. Lumber fire   92
13-3. Acid arrests   93
13-4. Simplify words   94
13-5. Rewrite sentences in active voice   95
13-6. Brief news (Write a 15-second spot)   95
13-7. News feature   95

14 *Web Writing*   96

    Teaching Suggestions   96
    Textbook Exercises
    1. Headlines and blurbs   97
    2. Personal essay   97
    3. Interviews – 1 cent   97
    4. Converting a story for the Web   98
    5. Web story   98
    Workbook Exercises
    14-1. Plan a Web project   98
    14-2. Headlines and blurbs   98
    14-3. Web briefs   99
    14-4. Chunk-style writing with cliffhangers   100
    14-5. Web news story   101

15 *Accuracy and Libel*   102

    Teaching Suggestions   102
    Textbook Exercises
    1. Corrections   103
    2. Actual malice   103
    3. Libel   103
    4. Privacy #1   104
    5. Privacy #2   104
    6. Search the Internet   104
    Workbook Exercises
    15-1. Libel quiz   105
    15-2. Libel quiz #2   107
    15-3. Online legal issues   107
    15-4. Legal scenarios   108

16 *Ethics*   109

    Teaching Suggestions   109
    Textbook Exercises
    1. Moral reasoning   110
    2. Student government candidate   111
    3. Anti-holocaust advertisement   111
    4. Online pornography   111
    Workbook Exercises
    16-1. The bad joke   112

16-2. The telephone number 112
16-3. Son of superintendent 113
16-4. A hero's private life 113
16-5. Anonymous sources 113
16-6. Cooperating with police 114
16-7. Personal dilemma 114
16-8. Code of ethics 114

17 *Multicultural Sensitivity* 115

Teaching Suggestions 117
Textbook Exercises 117
Workbook Exercises
17-1. Media survey 118
17-2. Photo Sensitivity 118
17-3. Gender stereotypes 119
17-4. Age perceptions 119

18 *Beat Reporting* 120

Teaching Suggestions 120
Textbook Exercises
1. Business feature 121
2. Specialty subject 121
3. Interview a beat reporter 121
4. Internet sources 121
5. List beats 121
Workbook Exercises
18-1. Beat story ideas 122
18-2. Briefs or press releases 122
18-3. Analyze beat coverage 122
18-4. Analyze a beat story 122
18-5. Team beats 123
20-6. Online newspaper beats 123
20-7. Analysis of beat resources 123

19 *Obituaries* 124

Teaching Suggestions 124
Textbook Exercises
1. Celebrity obituary 125
2. Jim Hensen obituary 125
Workbook Exercises

19-1. Basic obituaries — 126
19-2. Feature obituary - Jerry Garcia — 128
19-3. Online obituary — 130
19-4. Style quiz corrections — 130

20

Speeches, News Conferences and Meetings — 131

Teaching Suggestions — 131
Textbook Exercises
1. Burl Osborne speech — 132
2. Online speeches — 132
3. News conference: Richard Jewell remarks — 133
4. Online news conferences — 134
Workbook Exercises
20-1. Graduation speech — 134
20-2. Vonnegut hoax graduation speech - online — 135
20-3. News conference (Michael Jordan retirement) — 135
20-4. Meeting advance — 137
20-5. Meeting story — 138
20-6. School board meeting — 139
20-7. Style quiz corrections — 140

21

Government and Statistical Stories — 141

Teaching Suggestions — 141
Textbook Exercises
1. Figure your taxes — 142
2. Dream home — 142
3. Statistics: Vegetarians beware — 142
4. U.S. Census online research — 143
5. Campus budget follow — 143
6. Interactive quiz — 143
Workbook Exercises
21-1. Government and weather terms test — 144
21-2. Statistics – crime rates — 144
21-3. Weather statistics — 145
21-4. City budget story — 145
21-5. Online statistical profile of a community — 146
21-6. Caffeine consumption — 147
21-7. Style quiz corrections — 147

22 Crime and Punishment 148

Teaching Suggestions 148
Textbook Exercises
1. Crime story 149
2. Fire story 149
3. Court terms 151
4. Court hearing 151
5. Civil court case 151
Workbook Exercises
22-1a. Motor vehicle accident 151
22-1b. Burglary 152
22-2. Burglary 152
22-3. Fire fatality 153
22-4. Court terms quiz 155
22-5. Mummy saga 155
22-6. Campus crime statistics 157
22-7. Court cases 157
22-8. Style quiz corrections 157

23 Disasters, Weather and Tragedy 158

Teaching Suggestions 158
Textbook Exercises
1. Disaster coverage 159
2. First day airplane crash story 159
Workbook Exercises
23-1. Plane crash – Day 2 story 163
23-2. Explosion mainbar 163
23-3. Explosion sidebar 165
23-4. Coping sidebar 166
23-5. Basic weather feature 166
23-6. Covering grief 166

24 Profiles 167

Teaching Suggestions 167
Textbook Exercises
1. Newsworthy person 168
2. Vignettes 168
3. Celebrity profile 169
4. Coaching 169
5. Slice-of-life snapshots 169

Workbook Exercises

24-1. Autobiographical profile		170
24-2. Web autobiography		170
24-3. Background research for profile		170
24-4. Slice-of-life profile		171
24-5. Rosa Parks, Charles Kuralt or others		172

25 *Computer-assisted Journalism*   173

Teaching suggestions   173

Textbook Exercises

1. Occupations spreadsheet		173
2. Hate crimes spreadsheet		174
3. Population growth		176

Workbook Exercises

25-1. Sort and calculate #1		176
25-2. Sort and calculate #2		178
25-3. Write a story from statistics		180
25-4. Analyze data: Unmarried couples		180

26 *Media Jobs and Internships*   181

Teaching Suggestions   181

Textbook Exercises

1. Interview employers		182
2. Write about yourself		182
3. Cover letter and resume		182

Workbook Exercises

26-1. Research the organization		182
26-2. Interview graduates		182
26-3 to 23-5. Self explanatory		182

Appendix (Style tests)   183

Introduction

This Instructor's Manual is designed as a guide for use with the textbook and workbook. We all have different ways of teaching, and this manual is only meant to offer some ideas, not a prescription for instruction.

Despite all the exercises provided in the textbook and workbook, I confess that I am not a great fan of using exercises. Whenever possible, I prefer to send students out to cover breaking news or activities on campus or in the community. However, I believe the exercises can be of value if they are used to reinforce some of the writing concepts in the book. I use them mostly in class for writing and researching skills.

To help students gain reporting skills, I assign them to report and write a story outside of class weekly or every other week for more difficult stories. I also require them to submit weekly budgets of story ideas, which I review and suggest for their outside stories.

The book and workbook are based on the premise that students learn best by doing – and doing it immediately. I have had great success teaching students to report and write complete stories at the start of the semester rather than teaching them the individual parts first and then waiting until the middle or end of the course before assigning complete stories. Some of their initial stories may be very poor, but I firmly believe students will learn best by continued practice of gathering information and writing the stories without fear of failure. To this end, I use a "fail-safe" portfolio grading system, which I will describe in detail later in this introduction.

New material in this edition

At the request of professors who have used this textbook in the past, I have added more instruction about coaching in this introduction to the manual. Other new features:

- Web-related exercises and integration with online sources in almost every chapter. The textbook contains online coach boxes in every chapter.
- Many new exercises.
- A new chapter on Web writing.
- A revised chapter on sources with emphasis on online research.
- A new Web site with interactive self-graded exercises.
- A revised chapter on computer-assisted reporting.
- A completely new Web site with interactive exercises: *http://info.wadsworth.com/rich*

Organization of the manual

Each chapter begins with teaching suggestions for the textbook, followed by suggestions for using the textbook exercises and workbook exercises. The manual also includes examples of original stories on which some of the exercises are based and answer keys to the style quizzes and other exercises where applicable. Because the emphasis in this book is on teaching students to take risks, I prefer to tell students that the original stories are only examples of ways to write – not the right or wrong ways. In many cases the students' versions will be better than the original stories, which can be used for comparative analysis.

The textbook and workbook chapters contain far more exercises than you would need to reinforce the techniques in most lessons. I have tried to provide a variety of exercises ranging from simple to more difficult so that you can choose ones that suit your needs. In certain chapters, such as the chapters on speeches, meetings and news conferences (Chapter 20) and on crime and punishment (Chapter 22), I suggest that you give students some of the exercises orally so they can take notes instead of letting them read the information from the workbook exercises. After they have written their stories, they can compare their information and check for accuracy with the information provided in the exercises.

Style quizzes are provided at the end of several chapters in the workbook and are based on the exercises in those chapters. The style concepts that will be tested in each quiz are itemized under goals at the beginning of the chapter. To save time grading the style quizzes, you may find it easier to distribute the answers and let students grade their own papers as you go over the corrections orally. I usually correct the style quiz with students as soon as they take it to reinforce learning immediately. Additional interactive, self-graded style quizzes are on the Web site.

Although the book is designed to be taught sequentially, each chapter is self-contained in case you wish to teach specific chapters at any time during your courses.

The book is geared for use with beginning and advanced classes. In the advanced classes, I stress the first two sections of the book on reporting and writing process, but I skip the chapters on the basic news story, obituaries, speeches and meetings and some of the basic stories in the chapter on crime and punishment. Several of the chapters in the beginning of the book are brief, so I often assign two chapters a week. Because the skill levels in each class vary considerably, you may need to spend more time on some chapters than others, particularly in beginning level classes.

The Internet has made cross-disciplinary skills are more valuable as media fields continue to converge. In addition, some experience in other fields may be worth teaching to all students. I recommend that you teach Chapter 26, "Media Jobs and Internships," because students generally have no idea how to write a cover letter, and their resumes are filled with errors. Students need to learn how to market themselves for internships as well as for jobs. I usually teach this before the midterm so students have a chance to apply for internships and jobs before the end of the semester.

Coaching

Coaching is a way of teaching students to discover their strengths and weaknesses. It is not telling them what is right or wrong but rather, asking them leading questions and giving them tips to help them find techniques and a writing process that will work best for them.

Coaching vs. Editing Coaching differs from line editing for errors or improvements in the copy. Coaching should identify patterns of problems that students encounter in their writing and solutions. For example, if you notice that a student frequently starts leads or sentences with "There is" or "There are," you can discuss why this is a weak technique because "There" always takes a weak verb. Then you might discuss how to strengthen verbs if that seems to be a problem. Here are some coaching basic coaching tips:

- **Listen**

Establish a collaborative climate, not a confrontational one. Ask the student to discuss his/her strengths and weaknesses. Build on the person's strengths before proceeding to weaknesses.

Basic questions: Where are you struggling?

What works; what needs work?

- **Laud**

Always find something to praise. This can be something in a story or in past performance. Build on the positive before proceeding to the negative.

- **Limit**

Set only a few goals to accomplish at a time. Do not try to fix all the student's problems in one session. Limit the lesson. Be specific in suggesting remedies.

- **Reinforce**

Provide feedback. Praise any sign of progress; note any recurring weaknesses related to the goals you both are trying to accomplish. Remind the student of the goals and solutions you discussed when you grade the paper or in your next coaching session.

- **Reassure**

Make sure the student is aware that you are supportive.

- **Reward**

When the student achieves the goals, either fully or partially, reward him or her. It can be a note, a good grade or just verbal praise.

Approaches to Coaching

You can't always coach every student on every story. Here are some approaches you can take:

Coaching before reporting: Discuss the idea with the student reporter. Discuss any angles the student might be interested in developing and some information he or she should seek. Ask the student for ideas; do not dictate. Make this a collaborative discussion. Here are some questions for very quick coaching:

- What is the main news or issue that you expect to be discussed?
- How will this story affect readers?
- Are there any interesting, unusual or human angles you might pursue?
- Are there graphics or information boxes that you should consider?

Coaching before writing (5 to 10 minutes): This type of coaching can and should be done before the story is written. If you have only a few minutes, use the first three questions. If you have 10 or 15 minutes, you can pursue more questions.

- What is this story about? Ask the writer to state the main point in one clear sentence. That is the focus. If it isn't the lead, it should be stated as a nut graph – the main point of the story – and placed high in the story, preferably by the fifth paragraph. As a coaching tip, ask the writer to write this focus sentence at the top of every story. This will serve as a guide to help identify the focus. Everything else in the story should relate to this focus.
- What struck you as most interesting or important about this story? (That could be your lead or your focus)
- What about this story would make the reader care? (That's another point that could give you an idea for a lead or a key impact paragraph high in the story.)
- What are you considering for your lead? Praise if the lead sounds good. If the writer has no idea, ask some of the next few questions.
- Without looking at your notes, what do you remember as the most memorable point?
- What do you think the reader wants to know or needs to know? (List two or three key points. These will also help the writer determine an order for the story.)
- What order are you considering? The writer may not know, but the questions make the writer think about it. Ask the writer to jot down a few words to indicate the order.
- What graphics will accompany the story and how do they affect what you should put in or pull out of the story?

Coaching during the writing process: Walk around the classroom and ask students how they are doing and if they are struggling. Offer praise and encouragement when possible. If they are, offer help by coaching questions. Chances are that by asking the questions, you will be guiding students to find their own answers. If they need more help, offer suggestions. Some students may be very opposed to having you look over their shoulders as they write. If that is the case, ask them to feel free to come to you if they get stuck somewhere in the story. For other writers who welcome help, here are some suggestions. If they are struggling with the lead, ask any of the first three questions under coaching before writing. If they are having other problems, consider some of these questions:

- Where are you struggling?
- What are you trying to say? (Often the writer verbalizes the thought very well. If that is the case, offer praise and say, "Just write it that way."
- If the writer is having organizational problems, offer these questions:
- What questions do you think the reader might have at this point?
- What key words link you to the next thought? (Ask the writer to go back to the last paragraph for a clue about what should come next.)

As you can see, several of these questions are redundant. The questions just help the student think and talk about the story, and that is often the only help students need to discover their own solutions.

Coaching the class: Before and after students write their stories, I ask them some the leading questions: "What problems are you having reporting your stories?" or "Where did you struggle in the writing process?" Then we discuss those problems in class, and I often ask students to share techniques that worked well for them. If we have studied a process or specific techniques, I ask students if those techniques were helpful to them in their outside assignments.

Sometimes I will pair students and have them coach each other for about 15 minutes during class before they report or write their outside assignments. Students can ask each other: "What are you trying to say? What is the most interesting aspect of the story?" Then they can brainstorm ideas.

Team coaching: Another way of coaching is to team up two or three students on a story. They can interview sources together or split the interviews, if there are several sources, and share notes. Take about 15 minutes of a class period and ask the students to brainstorm ideas and discuss the reporting and writing strategy. When I use this approach, I circulate among the groups and share tips.

Coaching individuals: It is difficult to coach each student before he or she writes an outside assignment. Ideally I prefer to meet with each student every other week, but that has become impossible because of the large numbers of students. As a result, I urge students to call me or stop by during office hours to discuss their stories if they are having problems before they write them, but I only meet with them formally twice a semester to coach them and go over their portfolios as explained in the following part about grading. If you can handle the workload, it's ideal to coach students on their stories more frequently.

Portfolio Grading

Portfolio grading is an alternative to grading every paper a student writes. Although I edit all papers and write comments, I do not place grades on any of them. After the edited papers are returned, the students rewrite them and place all their stories – including class exercises and outside assignments – in a portfolio.

At midterm and again at the end of the term, I collect the portfolios with original and rewritten stories. At that time I evaluate the students with a form I use, and I have a conference with each student to discuss their grades. For beginning classes, I sometimes ask for portfolios three times during the semester. I cancel class for these coaching sessions and schedule students every 15 minutes. We discuss their strengths and weaknesses. I ask them where they are struggling, and I make suggestions for improvement.

The philosophy behind this grading method is that a student cannot fail a paper if he or she does the work. The student can always make it better by revising it. However, there are a few grounds for failure: plagiarism, a misspelled name or a factual error. I explain that in my syllabus. Plagiarism is punishable not only by failure but also by academic misconduct charges, which I will file against the student. The others errors can be corrected on the revised versions. Late papers automatically receive F.

If you prefer to grade each paper, I suggest giving equal weight to a rewritten version. But the non-graded method seems to encourage students to take risks. I stress that at any time during the semester if a student is concerned about his or her grade, the student may schedule a conference with me during office hours or come in any time I am available, and I will give her or him a progress report.

When the students submit their portfolios, I ask them to write a cover letter and a resume to a prospective employee (based on Chapter 26).

I have evaluated this grading method with students for the past 10 years and with few exceptions, students said the method encouraged them to take risks and helped them concentrate more on how to improve their papers than on their grades. There are always a few students who are very grade conscious and need to have a tangible sign of their grade. If I have any students who are in danger of failing or receiving a D grade, I usually schedule a special conference with them.

On the next page is the form I use to evaluate the portfolios, but you can tailor it to meet your own needs. (Leave spaces between categories for comments).

Please feel free to contact me at crich13@aol.com.

Evaluation Form

Ideas/story planning

Reporting
    Sources:

    Thoroughness:

    Quality of quotes:

    Accuracy:

Writing
    Focus

    Grammar/style

    Leads

    Organization .

    Creativity

    Pacing/flow

    Clarity

Overall strengths

Weaknesses/areas to improve

Grading key:
        A = Publishable quality
        B = Publishable with editing
        C = Substantial editing needed
        D = Marginal quality
        F = Unacceptable

Midterm grade:

Final grade:

Write From the Start: A Coaching Method

1

Goals

- To give students experience writing a news story
- To introduce the focus method of writing
- To create an awareness of the importance of graphics
- To teach Associated Press style for age, numbers, money and time.

This chapter sets the tone for the course. The purpose of this chapter is to simplify the writing process. The textbook and workbook activities are designed to give beginning students a chance to start writing on the first day of the course and to give advanced students a chance to refresh their skills.

Teaching Suggestions

This chapter may take one or two class periods to teach beginning students. The focus method used in this chapter is the basis for writing stories throughout the course. To help students find the focus, ask them to answer this question in a simple sentence: What's the story about?

Explain that this focus sentence can be their lead or their nut graph – the main point of the story. Students may be inclined to write a very broad focus statement, such as: This story is about a burglary. Help them narrow the focus to the most interesting or important angle. I ask students to put a focus sentence on top of all their stories throughout the semester.

Stress to students that once they get their focus, they must choose supporting material that relates to this central idea. Then discuss the tell-a-friend technique and ask students to use this concept to plan an order for their stories before they write.

If you want your students to begin writing on the first day of the course, you can assign one of the writing activities from the text or workbook. The graphics components may be taught in the next class period if you need more time. After I edit the stories, I find it helpful to give students a chance to revise them in class or for homework.

Coaching

As students are writing, walk around the room and coach them. If students are struggling with the process, help them identify their focus and check the order they have planned for their stories. If they are struggling with the lead, suggest that they use their focus sentence for their lead. Coaching this way gives students instant feedback. Sometimes it is more effective to let students start writing and make mistakes or struggle. Then as you walk around the room and observe common problems, you can interrupt the class and tell students how to improve their stories. Let them revise the stories they have started. It saves you time making comments on a lot of bad stories and gives students a chance to apply your suggestions immediately.

Although I recommend portfolio grading throughout the course instead of grading each paper, if you prefer to grade, I suggest that you don't do it on students' first stories. Students will pay more attention to your editing comments if they don't have to worry about a grade – at least initially. The coaching approach involved is that students cannot fail; they can revise anything that doesn't work well.

Textbook Exercises

1. Visual/verbal exercise

This exercise is designed to be written in a 50-minute laboratory period. Tell students to identify a focus and to think graphically. Some students may take less time. Suggest that students choose an interesting finding for the lead rather than a general statement that a study has been conducted. You may also encourage them to use a creative lead. Even students who have never written a news story tend to write catchy leads for this story. The Associated Press style concepts to teach with this story are ages, percents and numbers, which will appear in the style test at the end of the chapter in the workbook.

After students have written the story, discuss what facts they thought were interesting enough to be high in the story, and discuss their ideas for visuals. Graphic possibilities include a chart or facts boxes of the average life span of left-handed and right-handed people, percentages of left-handed people or the differences in gender and accident rates. Here is the original story that you may distribute so students can compare it with theirs.

Left-handers have shorter life span, research shows

SAN BERNARDINO — Left-handed people don't live as long as right-handers, according to research by a professor at California State University, San Bernardino.

A study of death certificates of more than 1,000 people in San Bernardino and Riverside counties, with questionnaires filled out by survivors, showed left-handers lived an average of nine years less than right-handers.

"The results are striking in their magnitude," said Diane Halpern, whose research was published Tuesday in the New England Journal of Medicine.

"The mean age of death for right-handed men and women was about 75. Left--handers died at about 66, said Halpern, a psychology professor.

There was another surprise when Halpern studied the deaths by gender: Left-handed women die around 72, while right-handed women die around 78.

For men, the difference was even more marked; Left handed men die about age 62; right-handers at 73.

Halpern said the research is the first to establish that left-handed people live shorter lives.

"We knew for years that there weren't many old left-handers. But researchers thought that was because in the early years of the century, most people born left-handed were forced to change to their right hands.

"So we thought we were looking at old people who used to be left-handed. But we weren't. The truth was, there simply weren't many left-handers left alive, compared to right-handers."

Halpern, a right-hander, doesn't believe that use of the left hand causes a risk of earlier death in itself.

"It's important that mothers of left-handed children not be alarmed and not try to change which hand a child uses. There are many, many, living old left-handed people."

But it could be that left-handedness accompanies other problems, she said.

Halpern said her research confirmed left-handed people have more accidents, presumably because the world is oriented to right-handers.

"Almost all engineering is geared to the right foot. There are many more car and other accidents among left-handers just because of their environment."

Frustration could elevate the left-handed person's stress level. The difficulties of adapting to a right-sided world might be a factor that causes a shortened life.

She said the study, done in conjunction with Stanley Coren of the University of British Columbia, must be interpreted cautiously.

"It should not, of course, be used to predict the life span of any one individual. It does not take into account the fitness of any individual," Halpern said. "And besides, some of my best friends are left-handed."

Marilyn Leary, *The* (San Bernardino, Calif.) *Sun.* Reprinted with permission.

2. Reaction story

This exercise is designed to help students begin interviewing people. Although you could students to interview any of their left-handed classmates, I prefer to have the interview strangers. You could assign this during a laboratory period or for homework. Tell students to ask specific questions about accidents or problems their left-handed sources have experienced. I have found that the sooner students start interviewing people, especially about something specific, the less anxiety they will have when they begin reporting for their own stories.

3. Online focus exercise

Discuss the questions in the text and encourage students to express their views. There are no right or wrong answers. This exercise is designed to get students to think about how print and online writing may differ and to prepare them for convergent media.

4. Find the focus

This is another way to reinforce students' understanding of the importance of finding a clear focus and to encourage critical thinking. If the newspaper stories do not have a focus high in the story, ask students if this discourages them from reading the story.

5. Online quiz

This self-graded, interactive quiz will help students identify focus and reinforce concepts in the chapter.

Workbook Exercises

1-1. Crime story

This exercise is helpful as a diagnostic tool to determine if students can pinpoint the most interesting information in the lead and if they have any creativity. Many students who are timid about writing may start with a simple summary lead about robbers escaping with $5,000. The more perceptive students will identify the focus as the baby's diaper saving the infant from a gunshot wound. The crime story also contains the race of the suspects. This is a possible discussion topic.

Class discussion questions: What did you find most interesting about this story: the fact that robbers escaped with $5,000 worth of jewelry or the fact that the baby's diaper prevented the bullet from hitting her? What do you think readers would find most interesting or unusual? Is the race of the suspects relevant? Should this be in crime stories? Compare your story with the original newspaper story.

The lead can be basic hard news or creative. Here is a student's lead:

Grace Ford has found a new use for diapers – bullet protection.

After two robbers broke into Ford's home and fired shots last night, she found a bullet hole in her baby daughter's diaper.

Here is the original story:

Diaper may have stopped bullet

TAMPA – An extra-thick diaper may have saved 10-month-old Brandi Ford from a bullet late Sunday.

Two armed, masked robbers burst into Brandi's home in Riverview at 11:30 p.m. and demanded money from the baby's mother, Grace Ford, 20, who was sitting in the front room with Brandi, who was in a playpen.

When the family's Rottweiler watchdog, Elka, began barking, the intruders fired three shots at the dog, sheriff's deputies said. All three shots missed the dog, but one bullet put a hole in Brandi's diaper.

When the baby began crying, her mother picked her up and found the bullet hole and the bullet.

"There was about an inch left to the diaper that it didn't pierce," Mrs. Ford said. "They were extra thick."

The robbers pushed Brandi, Mrs. Ford and her sister, Cynthia Phillips, 16, from room to room and took about $5,000 worth of jewelry, Mrs. Ford said.

Neighbors heard the shots and called sheriff's deputies, but the men got away in a car that investigators said had been waiting in a nearby cemetery.

According to sheriff's reports, both men were described as white, from 18 to 20 years old and of medium height and weight. One was wearing a ski mask and jogging pants with the letters "UF" (University of Florida) on the side. The other was wearing a white shirt and baseball cap.

Kathleen Ovack, *St. Petersburg* (Fla.) *Times.* Reprinted with permission.

1-2. Find the focus

These paragraphs are intended to help students identify a focus that is not too broad. Here are some suggested focus statements:

a. A study released today says people who abruptly quit drinking coffee may suffer effects of caffeine withdrawal.
b. A new law that went into effect yesterday in Maine requires employers to educate workers about sexual harassment.
c. A group of students at the University of _____ wants a concert by the Elvis Hitler band to be canceled because the students find the name offensive.
d. Two men were arrested on charges of drug trafficking after a police dog sniffed heroin in one of the man's sneakers.
e. Jason Gott received a postcard yesterday – 30 years after it was sent.
f. Use your local newspaper to find focus in stories. Discuss whether the stories have good focus. Whenever possible, use your local newspaper so the stories are more timely and relevant. However, if the newspaper is poorly written, use it to study why stories aren't clear, where the focus should be and other concepts.

1-3. Online focus: headlines and blurbs

It's not too soon to begin teaching students how to think for the Web. Although the book will emphasize writing for the Web in a separate chapter, this exercise will help students identify the focus and force them to think of focus in just a few words.

1-4. Visual elements

The visual exercises help students understand how graphic tools will affect their reporting and writing. Although copy editors usually write the facts boxes and words for other graphic tools, reporters need to learn how to gather information for graphics. Identifying pull quotes will help students determine what material from sources is worth putting in direct quotations and what information should be paraphrased. Here are some suggestions for information to include in the visual elements exercises:

a. Facts box: List the signs of frostbite
    Another facts box could be tips on what to do if you suspect you have frostbite.
b. Empowerment box: Where and when to register to vote
c. Pull quote: "It makes me sick in my heart to think we are still fighting for things we were fighting for 20 years ago."

1-5. Style quiz corrections

Corrections are in boldface type in parentheses.

1. A diaper saved a 10 month old **(10-month-old)** baby from a gunshot wound.
2. Grace Ford, a twenty year old **(20-year-old)** mother, said the robbers stole 5000 dollars **($5,000).**
3. 10-month-old **(Ten-month-old)** Brandi Ford was wearing an extra-thick diaper, which may have saved her life.
4. Grace Ford was sitting in her living room at 11:30 P.M. **(p.m.)** Sunday night **(eliminate night)** when robbers burst into her home.
5. The ten-month-old **(10-month-old)** baby was not harmed.
6. Right-handed females tend to live 5 **(five)** years longer than left-handed females. Right-handed males lived ten **(10)** years longer than left-handed males.
7. Residents may register to vote at the county clerk's office on Tuesday from 8 in the morning **(8 a.m.)** to 9 at night **(9 p.m.).**
8. Jason Gott received a postcard thirty **(30)** years late.
9. Even people who drink fewer than 3 **(three)** cups of coffee a day may suffer caffeine withdrawal if they abruptly quit drinking coffee.
10. Businesses in Maine that have more than fifteen **(15)** employees must educate workers about sexual harassment.

Changing Concepts of News 2

Goals

- To inform students about changes in the media
- To teach students how to think about new concepts of news and impact of the Internet
- To help students understand the importance of visual presentation
- To teach students the fundamental qualities of news
- To encourage students to begin using the Internet for research

Teaching Suggestions

This chapter can stimulate some interesting class responses, especially if you use the first workbook activity to kick off discussion about how the Internet is affecting newspapers and other media. If you have a laboratory with access to the Internet, ask students to call up media Web sites and discuss how they differ from print versions.

Here are some other suggestions:

- Ask students what newspapers and magazines they read regularly and what topics interest them. Ask students how much of their news they get from television vs. newspapers or the Internet. Ask them if they read news online, and if so, what sites they use regularly or what non-news sites they visit.
- Discuss the pros and cons of giving readers what they want vs. what they need.
- Ask students what they do or don't like about their campus or community newspaper, and discuss how these newspapers could be more responsive to various groups in the community. Ask students to recommend story ideas based on their views.

All these findings point to a need for better writing. Here are suggestions for teaching the activities and supplemental exercises:

Textbook Exercises

1. Reading experiment

This activity works better if the instructor brings copies of the campus paper or local papers to class rather than trusting students to bring their own. It's also better if you use newspapers they have not yet read. Ask students to place a check mark on the first item they look at in the newspaper. Then make sure students understand that you want them to read the paper for pleasure, not for a current events test. Have them place a check on the stories they start reading and an X when they stop. Give students five or 10 minutes to read the newspapers. After they have read the stories, discuss the first element they noticed. Chances are it will be a photograph, graphic or a headline.

This is a good kickoff for discussing the findings of the "Eye Trac" study about the importance of photographs and other visual tools. Stress that students must think about visuals when they conceive their story ideas. You may want to review some of the visual terms explained in Chapter 1, such as points of entry, facts boxes, and empowerment boxes. Discuss how most readers are scanners, especially online. Ask students how many stories they read all the way through and how many they just scanned. Discuss the kinds of stories that held their interest to the end. Many students say they don't read past the jump. This can lead to a good discussion about problems of jumps and the need to write tightly. Ask students to discuss the kinds of stories they liked and disliked.

2. Journal

After students have completed their journals, ask them if they were surprised by their own reading habits or by those of the people they interviewed.

3. Graphics

Ask students to discuss whether the local and campus newspapers provide enough graphics – maps, facts boxes, illustrations, photos. Ask what kinds of graphics they would recommend to improve the paper.

4. Brainstorm online news ideas

Take any story in a local or campus newspaper and ask students to discuss how it should be presented online. Ask students to brainstorm ideas for an online package for a holiday or campus issue.

5. Interactive quiz

Access this self-graded, interactive quiz online to test students' understanding of convergence and news qualities on the book Web site at: *http://info.wadsworth.com/rich*.

6. Test your news judgment

Students will enjoy this CNN quiz, which tests their news judgment against that of CNN editors. Encourage them to form their own opinions, which may differ from the conclusions on the quiz. Access the quiz on the book site for chapter 2: *http://info.wadsworth.com/rich*.

Workbook Exercises

2-1. Online news qualities

Discuss how online newspapers and magazines are affecting the print media. For example, increased pressures of competition on the Web are creating accuracy and credibility problems. You might ask students to discuss how e-mail and the Web have changed their lives. Encourage students to brainstorm how media will continue to change because of the Web and what features online publications can offer that print and broadcast media cannot.

2-2. Convergent Media

Assign small groups of three to five students and let them brainstorm ideas for present and future coverage in newspaper, television or magazine news. Discuss how convergent media operations affect their journalism education and the advantages/disadvantages they listed. Some convergent news organizations claim they get increased readership and exposure by partnerships between print and broadcast media. Convergence also creates a burden for journalists, who must increase their skills and add news coverage for online media.

2-3. Public (civic) journalism

Discuss the pros and cons of this form of journalism, especially as it applies to election coverage. Consider asking students to devise a civic journalism project based on important issues in your community. Encourage students to check the Pew Center for Civic Journalism online *www.pewcenter.org* or link to it directly from our Web site: *http://info.wadsworth.com/rich*

2-4. Qualities of news

Ask students to define the qualities of news in the items listed in this exercise. You can also ask them to read the front page and metro page of their local newspaper or their campus newspaper and identify which qualities of news the stories contain. Ask them to discuss why certain stories are on the front page and whether they would have selected different stories. Here are answers to the news quality exercise:

a. unusual, human interest
b. proximity, timeliness
c. helpfulness, timeliness, consumer
d. conflict, proximity, timeliness
e. celebrity
f. human interest, unusual
g. trend, possibly proximity

2-5. Hard-news and feature stories

This discussion could center on how qualities of news in hard news and features are often similar. Although feature stories may not be as timely as breaking news, timeliness is often a factor that students overlook. Discuss the importance of a nut graph in feature stories that tells readers why they are reading this story. Ask students to list a few hard-news and feature stories that would be of interest to readers in their area.

The Basic News Story   3

Goals

- To teach students the elements of a basic news story.
- To teach students how to use quotes and attribution.
- To reinforce style concepts of ages, percentages, addresses, money, numbers, titles, times, and geographical regions.

This chapter is designed to teach beginning journalism students the basic structure of a news story and how to use quotes and attribution from sources. You may also wish to use some of these exercises as refreshers for second-level reporting students.

Teaching Suggestions

You can reinforce the concepts in Chapter 1 by stressing that all news stories must have a single focus and elaboration of that central idea. With beginning students, you also may need to discuss the main questions any news story should answer: who, what, when, where, why, how and so what.

Although the idea of the inverted pyramid structure is implied in this chapter, it is more natural to explain the concept by telling students to put the most interesting information high in the story, particularly in these days of impatient readers and information overload.

Students are often confused about the difference between a lead and nut graph. Explain to them that if the lead tells the reader the main point of the story in the first sentence, it can serve the same purpose as a nut graph. If they choose to write a creative lead, they need a nut graph high in the story.

Another key point to stress is that the lead must be backed up with facts and quotes to support it.

You might find it helpful to have students read any story from their local or campus newspapers and analyze how it follows the basic structure of a lead, backup and supporting quotes or facts.

Although students often write better stories than the published versions from which these exercises were taken, you may distribute the original versions in this manual if you want students to compare them with their versions.

Quotes and Attribution

Beginning reporting students do not understand what should and should not be attributed. Explain the importance of attributing opinion and accusatory statements.

To help students decide what material should be in direct quotes, ask them to study the quotes in their local newspaper. Are some of the quotes boring or factual material that could be paraphrased?

Reinforce the idea of using "said" rather than synonyms, and explain the use or elimination of courtesy titles. However, it's helpful to note that most newspapers use courtesy titles in obituaries. Ask students to read a story in the local paper and note the use of "said" and how sources are referred to on second reference. This chapter also addresses punctuation of quotes.

Although terms such as "on the record" and "off the record" are discussed in the chapter on sources, the ethics box in the chapter introduces that concept. I urge students to make sure sources know they will be quoted at the beginning of an interview. Although some journalists disagree, I believe if a source says the comments are "off the record," the information should not be used.

Textbook Exercises

1. Basic news story

This is a brief story that students should be able to finish in class, preferably in less than 30 minutes. Before students begin writing, suggest that they use a list for some of the findings or ask them to consider what statistics they would put in a chart. Remind students to write out the word "percent" if you use AP style, although USA Today and some other newspapers use the symbol.

Here is a student's lead:

The next time someone brags to you about his or her sex life or income, there's a good chance the person could be lying.

A new study says that 90 percent of Americans lie about everything, including their sex life and income.

Here is the original story:

Lying is just a way of life

People "lie at the drop of a hat" about everything from the quality of dinner to whether they really love their spouse.

A new survey finds that 91% in the USA say they lie routinely. And 36% of those confess to dark, important lies.

The survey results are in the book "The Day America Told the Truth" (Prentice Hall), just arriving in stores.

When people do tell the truth, they voice things few want to hear: 51% say there's no reason to marry, 29% aren't sure they still love their spouse, 31% are having or have had an extramarital affair.

"Americans are willing to lie at the drop of a hat. Lying is part of their lives," says co-author James Patterson, chairman of J. Walter Thompson advertising agency.

"People say what others want to hear."

Trivial lies include insincere compliments on dinner or clothes. Dark lies are those that hurt others.

Other findings:

- 86% lie regularly to parents
- 75% to friends
- 69% to spouses
- 81% lie about their feelings
- 43% income
- 40% sex.

Karen S. Peterson, *USA Today*. Copyright 1991. Reprinted with permission.

2. Quotes and attribution

This exercise will help students determine the difference between factual material that does not need attribution and information that does. Let students discuss why they think attribution was or wasn't needed. Here are the answers to this exercise.

a. Not needed; factual statement
b. Needed; opinion
c. Needed; accusation (She has not been convicted of the crime.)
d. Not needed (If you are certain this is factual: If you were not there and had to get the information second-hand, you would need attribution.)
e. Not needed; factual statement
f. Needed; partial opinion (It's a fact that he died; the cause needs attribution.)
g. Not needed; factual statement (could require attribution, e.g. if you received information second hand and needed confirmation because this is a secret society, not a public meeting.)

3. Enterprise

Although it may be early in the semester, I believe it is important for students to gather information and write their own stories as soon as possible. Some students will do well, and others will turn in stories that are very poor. By giving them a chance to rewrite stories, you can encourage them to succeed. In most cases, students at this stage do not gather enough material to write a good story. You can use their papers to stress how they need to ask more questions, particularly how and why to gain more information.

4. Class Reunion Feature

This exercise serves several purposes: Students get to know their classmates, they get practice interviewing and gathering quotes, and they get experience writing a story from notes they have gathered. It also can reinforce the concept of accuracy in spelling names of sources. Encourage students to stand up as they interview people, so they gain note-taking experience as though they were reporting at a breaking news event. Although this exercise allows students to make up information, you can reinforce that in real situations, making up quotes is forbidden. I have used this exercise successfully in several classes, and my students have enjoyed it. I have also given automatic F's for misspelled names – a mistake students do not repeat if they receive this failing grade early in the semester.

5. Online Census Story

Encourage students to use lists for itemizing salary figures. This exercise also will give them experience in using numbers in stories. Stress that numbers can be boring if they are lumped together in paragraphs. You also can encourage students to search online for updated information on this topic.

6. Online textbook quiz

This interactive, self-graded quiz will reinforce concepts of focus, nut graphs and quotes and attribution. Access it under exercises on the book Web site: *http://info.wadsworth.com/rich.*

7. Basic news story 2

This exercise offers students another chance to write a basic news story. The information is on the book Web site and can be printed out. Access it under Chapter 3 at *http://info.wadsworth.com/rich.*

Here is a version that was published in the *Des Moines Register.*

ISU won't officially recognize heterosexual club, cites bias

A heterosexuals' club on the Iowa State University campus is angry because the university won't let it be a registered group.

University officials say the Heterosexual Society can't be a registered campus group because it discriminates against homosexuals, who can't be full members.

But Dee Backes, a senior from Decorah and member of the Heterosexual Society, says Iowa State's action impinges on her constitutional rights of free speech and freedom of association.

Lisa Norbury Kilian, assistant dean of students, said the university turned down the group because it has refused to admit homosexuals as full members. No registered campus group can discriminate on the basis of age, color, handicap, nationality, race, sex, religion, marital status or "affectational orientation."

Backes points out that homosexuals can join the group's two lower levels of membership but to be promoted to the top two levels, members must sign forms promising that they are straight.

Backes says she suspects the group already has a gay member in one of its two lower tiers of membership, although she believes he is a plant from one of the two gay campus groups.

The Heterosexual Society would bring in speakers, sponsor a heterosexual pride week and have other activities "to fight misinformation on homosexuals and AIDS, she says.

Although the group could carry out those functions without being a registered campus group, Backes says, "We want to be a registered group because we have the right to be one."

But Kilian says giving special membership privileges and rank to only particular members of a group because of sexual orientation is against ISU policy. Except for fraternities and sororities, which are allowed to discriminate by gender, no other group can exclude a particular group from its ranks.

Backes maintains that Iowa State is stepping on the heterosexual group's right of free speech and freedom of association.

Veronica Fowler, *Des Moines* (Iowa) *Register.* Reprinted with permission.

Workbook Exercises

3-1. Fire

This exercise is designed to test whether students can determine the most important element in their lead. If you want students to use a summary lead, suggest that they stress the impact on the people or the cause of the fire. Here is the original story:

Four families left homeless by Tacoma apartment blaze

Four families were left homeless after fire raced through an apartment complex in this Tacoma suburb, officials said.

No one was injured, but a pet cat died in the two-alarm blaze, firefighters said Monday. About 12 people had to be relocated.

The fire started yesterday in an upper corner unit at the Meadow Park Garden Court and spread to a two-bedroom apartment through a common attic, University Place assistant fire chief Lynn Wilbur said.

The blaze destroyed two units and damaged two others.

Rosemary Hurlburt, whose apartment was gutted, said she and her two daughters were at a convenience store when the fire started. The family lost a lot of new possessions, she said.

"We just got new stuff. My 5-year-old daughter just had a birthday party. We just got her a brand-new bunk bed set," Hurlburt said.

Investigators had not confirmed the cause of the fire, but Wilbur said the blaze may have been started by a stove that was left on in one unit.

"The pots were melted down on it," he said.

Apartment manager Steve Edwards said he couldn't relocate the families in the apartment complex because it was filled to capacity. Some of the residents may have to seek shelter through the American Red Cross, he said.

The Oregonian. Reprinted with permission.

3-2. Program advance

The point of this exercise is to help students avoid writing a lead saying "There will be a conference on date rape." Coach them on how they can choose information from a source for their lead by asking them what was an interesting fact that might entice the reader? You may also need to coach them on how to turn a quote into a statement for the lead so they don't just start with quote leads. Here is the lead on the original story:

At least one in four women will be sexually assaulted in their lifetime, and about 90 percent of college rape victims are violated by someone they know, said Sharon Danoff-Burg, graduate assistant in the Emily Taylor Women's Resource Center.

The statistics are part of the reason why she agreed to be one of four student panelists at the "Date Rape, Acquaintance Rape" forum tonight in the Kansas Union.

Delin Cormeny, *The University Daily Kansan.* Reprinted with permission

3-3. Online Version

If your students know how to search the Web, this exercise will teach them to start thinking about how print stories might be presented in online form

3-4. Burglary

This is a good exercise to determine how creative your students are   Some will write a creative lead and others may stick with a summary approach   Stress how either approach is acceptable but warn students not to be flippant about death or serious injuries   You also should stress how they should use quotes where they are appropriate, not strung together in huge blocks   This exercise may work with advance students as a refresher

Here are two leads from student papers
1   Roy L Jones has had some bad luck with his left leg   He has lost it twice in 30 years
2   Roy L Jones of Germantown returned to his car at the Shoney's restaurant at 811 Eastern Parkway Thursday to find that lunch had cost him more than he had planned

Here is the original story

Automobile break-in left
Louisvillian out of a limb

Roy L Jones is disgusted, but he says the thief who broke into his car Tuesday and took his $8,000 artificial leg must be just as repelled

Jones, 60, picked up his hip-to-floor prosthesis from the Falls City Limb and Brace Co , where it had been adjusted, then stopped to have lunch with a friend at Shoney's restaurant, 811 Eastern Parkway

Jones parked his 1990 Oldsmobile in the restaurant parking lot and left the leg wrapped in a plastic bag on the floor

Lunch lasted about 30 minutes, Jones said, and when he returned to his car, the back door was open, the glove compartment had been rifled and his leg was gone

"I'm disgusted as hell, is all I can say," Jones, of 950 Samuel St in Germantown, said yesterday   "I bet whoever took it, when they opened the package, is as disappointed as I am "

The leg had not turned up as of yesterday, nor has anyone been arrested for the theft, city police said

Jones said his leg is probably covered under his homeowner's insurance policy, but that gives him little consolation

"I just hate to go through all the hassle of getting another one made," he said   "You have to go down there for a fitting, then you have to go down there again "

Jones bought the artificial leg Dec 23 to replace one that was no longer usable   The new one was needed after his leg needed further amputation two years ago, he said

Jones said he lost his left leg more than 30 years ago in an industrial accident

He uses a wheelchair when he goes out, but the leg helps him move about his house

Louisville police Sgt Frank Lavender said Jones' misfortune drives home a point that police have been trying to convey to citizens – that it's not enough to lock your car

"We're trying to encourage people to look into their cars and see what's in there and put it in the trunk," Lavender said   "People need to be more careful "

Marvin Greene, *The*   (Louisville, Ky) *Courier-Journal* Reprinted with permission

3-5. Telephone bill

This exercise is designed to test students' creativity It works well with beginning and advanced students The focus is the high telephone bill If students have not grasped that, they have not mastered the concept of placing the most important factor in the lead or nut graph However, they may write a hard or soft news lead Remind them not to flood a lead with statistics, but they should back up the lead with the cost of the bill Here is the original story

The ring heard 'round the world

If you think your telephone bill last month was high, you should talk to Jim Tyler

Tyler's home phone bill for July was $110,099 44, with a late penalty of $1,650 27 after Sept 2

The amount of the bill – about a thousand times higher than what Tyler usually rings up – apparently is the result of illegal use of a credit card registered in his name

There were 3,261 calls listed on the latest bill, 44 of which are Tyler's The bill comprised 386 pages, was 1 3/4 inches thick and required postage of $2 90

The majority of the calls originated from coin-operated phones in the Boston area Calls had been placed to 53 foreign countries and to several locations in the United States, primarily along the East Coast

Tyler, administrator at the Lutheran Home care center in Herington, was expecting a higher-than-usual bill after receiving a call at 2 a.m July 27 from an operator asking if he would authorize a credit card call to China

"I said, 'No, I don't even know anyone in a foreign country,'" Tyler recalled

The operator then informed him several calls to foreign countries had been made using his credit card number during the past several hours and that he could expect an astronomical phone bill

"By astronomical, I thought maybe $2,000 or $3,000," Tyler said

The calls of longest durations were from Boston to China The granddaddy of them all was a seven-hour (420 minutes) marathon call that began at 10 36 p m on July 26   The billing charge was $690

The operator reassured Tyler he wouldn't be responsible for paying for the calls to foreign countries or locations in the United States that neither he nor family members had made

Tyler said he hadn't totaled the amount he actually owes to Southwestern Bell Telephone Co

He said he thinks the credit card number was stolen when his daughter, Trisa, placed a call last summer from a coin-operated phone in a Pittsburgh, Pa , airport

Trisa was returning from a church group trip to Kentucky when she tried to call home There was no answer

However, Tyler said someone at the airport apparently saw her punch in her father's credit card number Tyler said he thinks the number was then sold several times

The Topeka (Kan)Capital-Journal Reprinted with permission

3-6. Quotes

This exercise is designed to help students decide what information should be in direct quotes and what should be paraphrased or not attributed at all Here is the corrected version

Package Arrives -- 25 Years Late

WASHINGTON (AP) -- A package from New York City to a Washington address finally arrived – albeit more than 25 years late

"The package containing three 16 mm reels of the 1954 movie classic 'On the Waterfront,' that was mailed July 3, 1974, was delivered Saturday to a town house in Northwest Washington," authorities said *(This statement does not have to be in quotes It is factual and it is not interesting enough for a direct quote But "On the Waterfront," a title, needs double quote marks)*

"The addressee, Martin Brinker of the District Living Cooperative, no longer lives there " *(Same explanation, the statement is a fact, no quote necessary)*

The package instead was left with Jason Ferguson, a 22-year-old George Washington University student

"I'm going to grow up and graduate from college in less time that it took the U S Postal Service to deliver this," Ferguson said " I would really like to think it's a hoax, but it doesn't look that way " *(The last two sentences should be in quotation marks - first person reference)*

Postal Service spokesman Gus Ruiz said while things like this occur, they don't happen very often   "When they do, we have the same question, 'Where was it?'" *(This is correct, a single quote mark should be after the question mark, then a double quote as it appears in the exercise)* he said

Ruiz speculated because the films were shipped parcel post, they could have "been lost" (Remove these quote marks - bad partial quote) either on a train or a bus

"The package could have been stored in a holding area until their discovery," he said *(quote acceptable but not necessary)*

The films were sent insured by the Audio Film Center of Mount Vernon, N Y Brinker apparently rented the film for $24 and the invoice warned him to "return promptly after use to avoid overtime charges " *(quote acceptable but could be eliminated)*

Adapted from a story by The Associated Press   Used with permission

3-7. Punctuating quotations

This exercise will give students practice with punctuation   Remind them to put commas and periods inside quotation marks   This is the most common error   Here are the corrections

A bar is an unlikely place to meet someone you will marry, **(add comma)** according to a researcher at the University of Chicago

Philip Schumm, one of the researchers of a sex study, said, **(add comma)** "No more than 4 percent of dates that begin at a bar end up in marriage **(Eliminate quotation marks at the end of this sentence because quote continues)**

"The most common way of meeting a partner is the most ordinary way," said Schumm, a research associate at the University of Chicago   "Someone you know introduces you to someone they think you would like". he said. **(no quote, no attribution because the quote continues, and the previous sentence had attribution)** "That's the best way to meet someone " Schumm said. **(Again, eliminate quote at start of sentence and cross out the attribution End sentence with a period)**

Schumm and other Chicago social scientists wrote a book, "The Social Organization of Sexuality," **(comma inside quotation marks)** which says that Americans are more conservative about sex than previous studies showed

Early sex leads to failed relationships, **(add a comma)** the researchers said   Only 2 percent of couples who had sex in the first two days of their relationship ended up getting married, the researchers said

"I guess you could say this sheds some light on the limits of the casual pickup," **(comma inside quotation marks)** Schumm said

Adapted from a story by the McClatchy News Service

3-8. Style quiz corrections

This quiz emphasizes age, titles, numbers, writing out "percent," money, addresses, regions, when to use U S versus United States and time You can have students take this as an open book test using the Associated Press Stylebook, or you can ask them to take it as a test   I recommend correcting it in class so students can get instant feedback Corrections are in boldface type

1 The police officer in charge of the investigation was Sergeant **(Sgt)** Frank Lavender
2   The woman's daughter was just five **(5)** years old
3 Fire officials said that twelve **(12)** people had to be relocated because of the fire
4 The survey showed that ninety % **(90 percent)** of the American people lie routinely
5. The artificial leg cost the man 8,000 dollars **($8,000)**
6 The 60 year old **(60-year-old)** man lives at 950 Samuel Street **(St)** in Louisville
7. Jim Tyler's phone bill last month was 110 thousand dollars and 44 cents **($110,000 44)**
8 Most of the telephone calls were to places along the east coast **(East Coast)** of the U S **(United States)**
9 Tyler said 3261 **(3,261)** calls were on the bill, which required postage of two dollars and ninety cents **($2 90)**
10 One of the calls was placed at 5 51 P M **(5:51 p m)** on July 27 and another was at 8:00 A M **(8 a m)**

Grammar and Usage 4

Here are the answers to the textbook exercises in Chapter 4 Corrections are in parentheses

Goals
- To reinforce the importance of grammar and style
- To give students practice in correcting common grammar and style errors

Teaching Suggestions
This chapter is based mostly on tests You might enjoy checking out the interactive grammar exercises linked to the Web site for this book
http //info wadsworth com/rich

Textbook Exercises

1. Grammar A-K

a She felt bad (correct) about missing the school board meeting, but her editor fired her ~~irregardless~~ (regardless) of her excuse

b We will all join ~~together~~ in prayer for the students who died in the shooting, and we will fly the flags at ~~half-mast.~~ (half-staff)

c It's ~~alright~~ (all right) if you miss class for a job interview, (semicolon or period Capitalize you if you use a period)you can make up the test tomorrow

d. We'll divide the workload ~~between~~ (among) three students

e. The St Joseph Board of Commissioners ~~are~~ (is) planning to submit a proposal for a bond issue to pay for road improvements, and they are hoping the election committee will reach a consensus ~~(of opinion)~~ to put the issue on the ballot

f I know you are ~~anxious~~ (eager) to get this job, but each of the applicants will have a chance to discuss ~~their~~ (his or her) strengths and weaknesses with the personnel director

g Based on your writing skills, it looks ~~like~~ (as if or as though) you could be a good journalist

h Each of the students is (correct) going to receive a plaque with ~~their~~ (his or her diploma) diplomas at graduation

i She was so embarrassed (correct) that she had ~~less~~ (fewer) than five answers correct on the quiz

j After the boss read the report, he gave it to Jim and ~~I~~ (me) to rewrite and said ~~its~~ (it's) due back by Monday

2. Grammar L-Y

a. The people ~~that~~ (who) attended the gay rights rally said it was ~~one of the most unique~~ (a unique event) ~~events~~ the school had sponsored

b. However, the participants in the rally said the media ~~was~~ (were) annoying when they converged on the speakers with cameras and microphones

c Some of the speakers felt ~~badly~~ (bad) that the crowd became unruly, (insert comma) and the organizer said he was embarassed when some of the participants complained

d. ~~Needless to say,~~ (eliminate) Next year the rally will be planned better

e. None of the five students involved in the fracas is (correct) going to be punished

f The first-place award, ~~that~~ (which) was an engraved silver bowl, was received by the class valedictorian

g. The three top ~~restauranteurs~~ (restaurateurs) in the city provided food for the banquet, but ~~over~~ (more than) 200 people got sick after the event

h. The City Board of Health, ~~that~~ (which) investigates such cases, said the food smelled and tasted ~~well,~~ (good) but ~~they are~~ (it is) withholding judgment on the cause of the illness until the food can be tested

i. ~~Irregardless, alot~~ (Cut irregardless   A lot or Many people) of people were ~~laying~~ (lying) on the ground, holding their stomachs in pain

j. The city health inspector wanted to know ~~who~~ (whom) he should blame, and he said he was moving ~~towards~~ (toward) a solution to the mystery of revealing ~~whose~~ (who's or who was) responsible for the food poisoning outbreak

3. Edit a Story

The errors are underlined, and corrections are in parentheses

In 1918 William Strunk Jr produced a little book for his English course at Cornell University, (insert period Capitalize It) it had a great affect (effect) on his students   E B White, one of the students who (whom) the professor taught, published the book in 1957   Today the book, that (which) was originally known as "The Little Book," is still having a great effect (effect is correct) on writers   Its (It's) called The Elements of Style   Like I said, (As I said,) it's still popular, and every writer should have their (his or her) own copy   It's presently (currently) available on the World Wide Web

Strunk never thought it was ~~alright~~ (all right) to use ~~alot~~ (a lot) of unnecessary words One of his famous sayings ~~are~~ (is) "Omit needless words". (period inside quotation marks) Between you and ~~I,~~ (me) that advice is still good today, and I feel ~~badly~~ (bad) that this story is filled with errors that ~~would of~~ (would have) made Strunk cringe ~~It goes without saying~~ (cut this up to that) ~~that~~ Strunk would

21

have been ~~embarrased~~ (embarrassed) if I ~~was~~ (were) in his class None of these sentences ~~are~~ (is) perfect, and if this ~~was~~ (were) the way a student wrote, Strunk would have issued stern ~~judgement.~~ (judgment)   Poor grades ~~were received~~ by students who wrote this badly (Reword last sentence to active voice Students who wrote this badly received poor grades)

—— ~~Their~~ (There) is no excuse for writing badly, Strunk might have said "Vigorous writing is concise~~"~~,~~ (insert comma before quotes) Strunk wrote The media ~~does~~ (do) not always follow Strunk's advice   He was the ~~most unique~~ (a unique teacher in his time, but not most unique) teacher of his time If ~~your~~ (you're) ~~anxious~~ (eager) to be a good writer, you'll check out his book online at this site

< http //www bartleby com/141/ >

Workbook Exercises

4-1. Active vs. Passive Voice

a passive
b. active
c active
d. passive

4-2. Action Verbs vs. Linking Verbs

a. There was an increase in tuition costs last year in universities throughout the nation   Tuition costs increased last year in universities throughout the nation
b There is a demand for technology that contributed to the increased tuition A demand for technology contributed to the increased tuition
c. There is new legislation that reduces the interest rates on federally backed student loans New legislation reduces the interest rates on federally backed student loans
d There are many students who need to improve their grammar skills before they can become good writers Many students need to improve their grammar skills before they can become good writers
e. There were 17 students who attended the lecture, but there were many others who decided to stay home because of the inclement weather   Seventeen students attended the lecture, but many others decided to stay home because of inclement weather

4-3. Dangling Modifiers

Several alternatives are possible
a. Carrying his books in his backpack, the strap broke
    As he was carrying his books in his backpack, the strap broke (or)
    Carrying his books in his backpack, he noticed that the strap broke
b. When planning a meeting, you should have an agenda
c. While discussing the election, the people engaged in heated debate over the
    topic of privacy and politicians
d. Living in a small town for many years, he was overwhelmed by the large
    population of this city
e. After spending three hours in the library, he thought the number of books seemed
    endless

4-4. It's, Its

a. It's
b. its
c. it's
d. its
e its

4-5. That, Which

a which (set off the clause in commas)
b. that
c which (set off clause in commas)
d which (set off clause in commas)
e. that (assuming there are other computer labs)

4-6. Who or Whom

a   The person who is in charge of hiring is the one whom you should contact
b.   Whom do you plan to see when you go for your job interview?
c.   These are the officials who will make the decision about whether your organization
gets the money
d.   Do you know who is in charge of the event?
e.   I don't know who was responsible, but whoever stole the fraternity mascot will be
caught

4-7. Run-on sentences

a run-on period after credit card
b correct as is
c. run-on period or semicolon after contested
d. run-on period after Sweden
e run-on Change to
    More than 60 people were killed and 173 others were injured, (cut comma) when
    flames erupted in the dance hall filled with teen-agers Or use a semicolon
    between killed and 173

4-8. Subject-Verb Agreement

a. is   **b.** expects   c are   d is   e wants

4-9. General Usage

a. The media are often blamed for poor coverage of politics
b. The student felt bad after she took the test
c. I am eager to get a new job
d. He thought it was all right to turn his paper in a few days late
e. The Board of Education met last night, and it plans to resume discussion of the proposal next week
f. Some people thought the president's behavior was embarrassing
g. Each of the board members knows what he or she must do
h. How much farther do we have to go before we reach the lake?
i. If I were in your position, I would quit
j. None of the women in the class was planning to go on to graduate school
k. It's clear that the argument was between him and his wife
l. The date for submitting the advertising campaign was not going to work out for either him or his boss
m. Give the free pizza to whoever shows up first
n. Do you know who hit the most home runs?
o You never know whom you will run into when you go to the cafe
p I know I laid the book on the table last night, but it disappeared
q. You should have used better judgment
r. None of you is going to graduate this spring
s. He was planning to become a restaurateur
t. The journalism school, which is on K Street, is the building with the green roof
u Whom did you send your resume to when you mailed it last week?
v. If you lose the election, you can run again next semester
w. If I were in a better mood, I'd let you skip this test
x Fewer than five students showed up for the presentation
y. The disagreement is strictly between you and me, so I don't think you should ask your brother to intervene
z. If you studied a lot of these items in your textbook, you should do well

Curiosity and Story Ideas 5

Goals

- To teach students how to find story ideas
- To teach students how to use curiosity as a reporting tool
- To teach students how to use their observations in reporting and writing
- To help students think visually when planning stories
- To teach students how to use press releases as a basis for ideas
- To teach students to use the Internet for story ideas
- To help students understand ethical problems of conflict of interest

Many students are under the impression that their employers will assign all their stories It is important to stress that editors in all areas of the media expect employees to devise many of their own story ideas A good story begins with a focused, newsworthy idea Beginning students often devise very broad story ideas that will be difficult to develop when they gather information Although you may prefer to assign specific story ideas for some parts of the course, it is important for students to learn how to conceive their own ideas

This chapter provides important training for many of the writing techniques in this book, particularly the show-in-action descriptive techniques for news and feature stories Many students believe that their news stories must be based only on what sources say, and they do not understand how to weave their observations into a story Students need help developing their curiosity as well as their observation powers The techniques in this chapter also help students improve their reporting skills This chapter is also fun to teach

Check our Web site for this book at *http //info wadsworth com/rich*

Teaching Suggestions

I require my students to submit a weekly budget of three story ideas Some semesters I assign students to campus or city beats, from which they must base their story ideas I review students' budgets to determine if their story ideas are workable and suggest the ideas I think are best I return the budgets to students the next class period and give them a week (or two) to write a story about one of the ideas from their budgets The budgets are cumulative, so students may choose an idea from any of their budgets rather than only from the one submitted the week before their next story Some students do a great job and others struggle

Remind students to list a graphic idea – a photograph, chart or illustration – for each budget item Some weeks I specify that the budget must contain ideas for a meeting, speech, profile or other topic to correlate with the material I plan to teach in class Reviewing their story budgets takes very little time and saves a lot of time editing poorly conceived stories

I recommend that you ask your university public relations department to put you on the mailing list for press releases You can use some of these releases to help students who have weak story ideas

To teach this chapter, demonstrate the concept of mapping by brainstorming ideas with students, such as weather stories or topics for news stories in your area, and map the story ideas on the board If you want more active participation from all students, place students in small groups and have each group map several ideas related to a topic Some topics suited to mapping include parking problems, overcrowded classes, sexual harassment, affirmative action, underage drinking, increased school fees and budget cutbacks

If you have a campus directory, scan it for unusual departments or clubs and distribute copies of a few pages to students Then ask them to find entries that sound unusual or interesting enough for story ideas

Training students to be observant is fun. One observation activity I have used with great success involves asking students to describe an object that should be very familiar to them A wall-length photograph adorned the entrance of the University of Kansas journalism school where I taught for 11 years Students passed it every day on their way to the reporting laboratory I asked students to describe the mural, which shows the *Emporia Gazette* newsroom of William Allen White, for whom the school is named Silence, then giggles ensued because most of the students didn't have a clue I've used a similar situation at the University of Alaska The exercise has shock value to show the students how unobservant they are If you have a similar landmark or obvious item that students should be aware of at your school, try this exercise

If it is possible for students to get published in the campus newspaper, I recommend that you encourage them to devise ideas for stories they can submit for publication I am convinced that whenever students have a real opportunity to be published, they do a better job on their stories and their motivation increases

I use online resources extensively to help students gain ideas and background for stories It's important to stress that students should not take information from online stories without attribution Plagiarism of Web materials is rampant, and students don't always understand that copying material from online sources is just as illegal and serious as copying from print sources I ask them to list the URLs of related Web sites in their budgets and stories

Ethics: The ethical dilemma in the textbook concerns conflict of interest It's a good idea to let students know early on that they should not be writing about friends or organizations to which they belong because they will not be able to write a balanced story This issue often comes up when students propose story ideas

Textbook Exercises

The textbook exercises are self-explanatory Many of these exercises help students become more observant in reporting The exercises also help them develop feature leads based on show-in-action techniques I particularly like the walking tour, especially when the weather is pleasant I tell my class of 20 students that we should gather at least 30 to 40 story ideas by the end of the 50-minute class period In place of the campus walking tour, you might take a walking tour of any part of your community, such as the downtown business section or any other area where you think students could easily find ideas

Workbook Exercises

Discussion of models or specific answers for these exercises can vary according to your class and your location

5-1. Coaching

Ask students to work with a partner and coach each other on a story idea as directed

5-2. Three ideas in 15 minutes

This is similar to the textbook walking tour, but easier and faster to do as a class exercise   It reinforces the concepts of teaching news qualities and basic news because students have to gather items that are newsworthy   I require them to write up their ideas as news briefs so they can gain practice writing a lead and gathering the crucial information

5-3. A-Z brainstorming

Kathy English, a former journalism professor at the Ryerson Polytechnical Institute in Toronto, Canada, offered her students a "dictionary of subjects" from A to Z with story suggestions   Students can brainstorm ideas for each or some of these words   Here are some of them
Accidents – Avoiding daily risks, the most dangerous hour or places
Accounts - What your budget should tell you
Agriculture - The decline or success of certain types of farming (locally), farming as a career, the woman farmer, and so on
Cold – How to cure one, coldest spot in Canada
Fear – How to be self-confident
Name - How to remember names, how you got your name
Road – What a road costs, busiest roads, prettiest roads
You could even make students devise their own list of A to Z words and ideas
Other possibilities are to place students in teams of three or four and let them work together on a project   They can brainstorm ideas, and each student can develop a different story for the project or they may all do the same one by sharing notes and resources. It also allows them to coach each other and work in a team setting, which is gaining in popularity in newspapers

5-4. Localize national news

This exercise is more effective if you ask students to bring newspapers to class and ask them to find local angles to current national news or click into online news sites   It also encourages students to read the newspaper and check news Web sites

5-5. Special sections

Even if you don't get a chance to produce special sections for your local or campus newspaper, this exercise can be valuable for brainstorming, especially if you have several public relations students who may be producing these kinds of materials on the job.

5-6. Classified advertisements

The workbook ads can be a start for discussion, but it is preferable to have students read your campus newspaper for ideas. Ask students how they would develop the stories from the advertisements and what sources they would seek.

5-7. Plan an online newspaper

This exercise also works best if you divide the class into small groups so they have more interaction. Save the last 15 minutes of the class period for discussion of each group's ideas. If you do this as a class discussion, eliminate the directions for writing a plan. Stress how the online site should differ from a print site. Emphasize the use of interactive elements, which set the Web apart from print media.

5-8. Curiosity training

Getting students to brainstorm questions about news events can be effective in class with students working in groups or just for discussion purposes. You could have students write their questions and then discuss them to make sure everyone is involved. Substitute any questions you like, especially questions about a recent news event in your community.

5-9. Descriptive writing from observation

The point of this exercise is to teach students how to select relevant details instead of flooding their writing with adjectives or details that do not advance a story. Give them an example, such as a stuffed teddy bear on their bed or favorite records and posters. Ask what those objects reveal about the person. Ask students to be specific when they describe objects, such as who or what is in the poster, what color is it, what size is it, and so on.

5-10. Analogies

Ask students to write analogies for things they observed on campus or people they know. Explain how analogies based on observation can enhance writing.

Sources and Online Research **6**

Goals

- To teach students how to find sources
- To teach students to develop multicultural sources
- To teach students how to find and use records
- To teach students how to use the Freedom of Information Act
- To teach students to use the Internet for research

Teaching Suggestions

Teaching students how to find sources is easy. Getting them to use many sources in their stories is more difficult. My students tend to be so grateful that anyone will talk to them that they usually stop short of finding additional sources for their stories. To help students find sources, stress the matchmaker technique of having one source recommend other people. Emphasize that students should get other points of view, particularly in stories involving conflict. If one source says something about another person, students need to know they should try to reach that other person for comment.

You might require them to have two or more sources for every story. However, when they are doing features or reaction stories, emphasize that students should choose quotes carefully and not use repetitive quotes just because they come from different sources.

Another important portion of this chapter acquaints students with public records. If possible, take students to your local government offices and have them search for public records mentioned in the text. My former colleague, Mary Wallace, teaches her students how to find records by assigning each student to a different office in the city or county.

Each student must find out what records are available in his or her assigned office and write a report. Wallace then compiles their reports into a booklet and distributes this "source book" to the class. It's a valuable learning experience and a good resource to have on hand for future classes. You may prefer this alternative to the individual record searches suggested in the textbook. Students are required to name the directors and the location of each office, write about the responsibilities of each office and report about what records are available. In addition, students must suggest a few story ideas to be generated from reports and functions of each office.

A major part of this chapter and workbook deals with how to search and use online records, which are now readily available but not always reliable. Students need to know how to check the credibility of online information.

Federal Documents

Many universities and public libraries serve as depositories for federal documents. Regional depositories receive all the materials available from the federal government; local depository libraries receive selected documents. If you have a regional depository library in your university or city or a local one with enough documents worth a class trip, take students to the library and ask the librarian for a tour. These libraries have a different coding system from regular libraries, and help from the federal documents librarian is almost essential.

You might assign students to write a news story based on a federal document, such as a congressional hearing, a report or anything else they find of interest. Let students browse though old documents and let them choose their own topic so they can get an idea of how much is available. Suggest that they use yesterday as their time frame, as though the hearing or report is a current news story. Many of these records are available online, and students should be aware of them. Links to many online resources are on the book Web site: *http://info.wadsworth.com/rich.*

Textbook Exercises

1. Cross directory

This lesson is fun to teach, especially if you make a game of the cross directory exercise. You can use printed cross directories or Internet research. If you have several cross directories in your library, bring them into class. Place students in groups of three or four. Write the name of a person (a city or university official or anyone you choose from the directory) on the board. Ask students to find the person's telephone number and address in the directory, using the basic portion of the directory that is similar to a regular telephone book. Then ask them to find the person's neighbors by using the address portion of the book. Another part of the exercise is to give students telephone numbers you have selected from the directory and ask them to identify the people to whom those numbers belong. To make this a game, ask students to raise their hands when they have found the information you request. The first group that finds the information wins.

To do this exercise on the Internet, start with a basic people search engine such as yahoo.com or infospace.com and find the person's address and phone number. Then use a reverse directory at infospace.com or others to find other people in the neighborhood by typing in just the address.

2. Databases

If you have access to databases, choose a topic suggested in the textbook or one you prefer. Ask students to find two stories and get printouts, and list experts they may contact. It may suffice to take students to the library and show them how to use the databases, especially if there are hefty fees involved. If you have access to Lexis-Nexis, encourage students to learn how to use this.

3. Reports

The best way to show students the police reports is to ask your local or campus police department to give you a few. Police officials may be reluctant to provide a copy of a real report. You can demonstrate this exercise even if they cross out the names of the victims or suspects. Less preferable, but of some instructional value, is the alternative of providing students with a blank police report and asking them to fill it out, making up the information or using information you give them.

4. Record search

This exercise can be done through records in your local government or online. Start with a people search engine such as Yahoo.com or Infospace and see if the community has online property records. It's best to check property records in your local courthouse. Make arrangements with the county clerk, director of the Register of Deeds office and officials in the courthouse. Before assigning this activity, it helps to take the students through a tour of the county offices where they can find these records. If you prefer, have all students research the background of one individual instead of choosing their own subject. That way, you might put the needed records on file.

The following is a sample record search that you may distribute to students as an example. The student who conducted this search investigated a state senator. She visited the house to get the description of the outside, but the description of the home's inside comes from land records. Information on campaign contributions is on file in the state or county office.

The quiet tree-lined residential street in historical old Lawrence echoes thoughts of days gone by. The large two-and-a-half story masonry and frame house at 737 Indiana Street was built in 1906 and belongs to Winton Allen Winter Jr. and Mary Boyd Winter.

The dark brown-shingled house with white trim sits across three lots in the middle of the block. The stone foundation and plaster walls are reminiscent of homes built around the turn of the century.

A swing set and fenced play area in the back yard make a perfect place for their three daughters – Katie, Molly and Elizabeth – to play. A drive off the rear alley leads to a detached garage. Two speedboats sit behind the garage, covered for protection from the winter months and awaiting the family's summer fun.

The house has nine rooms, including five bathrooms, a family room, and two and one-half baths as well as an attic and full basement. Carpet covers the majority of the house, which is cooled in the summer by central air and heated in the winter with gas.

Winton and Mary Winter are the third owners since 1934 of the Indiana property in the Lane's First Addition. They bought the property from Richard A. Barber, an agent and power of attorney for Jane Barber, et al. The deed was recorded on Jan. 23, 1986.

They have two outstanding mortgages on the property, totaling $100,000. The first, for $75,000, is with Standard Mutual Life Insurance Company and was taken out on Dec. 3, 1986. The second, for $25,000, is with People's National Bank and was taken out June 1, 1988. They pay $62.50 per year to the state for mortgage registration.

Reappraisal in 1990 increased the assessed value of the home $18,300 from $142,600 to $160,900. The land is valued at $15,900. With the tax rate in Lawrence at 125.80 mills (a mill equals $1 per every $1,000 of assessed property value), last year Winter paid $2,669.48 in taxes, based on 12 percent of the market value — $21,220.

Winter and his wife jointly own a 1988 Dodge and paid $555.46 in Douglas County property tax last year. A 1979 Chevrolet is registered in Winton's name, and he paid $37.86 in property tax last year. Their insurance company is West America Insurance Company.

Winton was born April 19, 1953. His father was Winton Allen Winter Sr., also of Lawrence. The elder Winton was born Aug. 20, 1930 and served in the Korean War and received the Korean Service medal. The younger Winton is married to Mary Boyd Winter, who was born Nov. 24, 1953. Both are registered Republicans and belong to Alvamar Country Club.

Winter received his B.S. degree from the University of Kansas in 1975 and his J.D. in 1978. He is an officer, director and stockholder in the Lawrence law firm of Stevens, Brand, Lungstrum, Golden and Winter, located in the First National Bank Building on Massachusetts. He is a director and stockholder of Winter Land and Cattle, Ltd., Ottawa.

First appointed to the Kansas Senate in 1982, he was elected in 1984. In the 1988 general election he defeated Democrat Michael C. DuPree with 67 percent of the vote. Winter received campaign contributions in 1988 totaling $23,909 and had expenditures of $20,748. The total political committee, business and union campaign contributions were $12,225.

Since becoming a state senator, Winter has served as chairperson of the Economic Development and Special Claims Against the State committees. He has been vice-chairperson of the Governmental Organizations committee and a member of the Judiciary, Local Government, State Building Construction, and Ways and Means committees.

In addition to being a member of the American Bar Association, Winter is on the board of directors of the Boys Club of Lawrence, Lawrence United Fund and The Shelter, Inc. He is a member of the Chamber of Commerce, Kansas Bar Association, Kansas University Alumni Association and Rotary Club.

By Bonnie Short. Used with permission.

5. FOIA request

You may choose a particular agency or ask students to research the name of the agency and appropriate officers. If students plan to mail their letters, you need to check to make sure several students are not requesting the same material. The activity is effective if students just have to do preliminary research and write the letters, even if they are not planning to mail them.

6. Enterprise story

This story combines research and interviews and can test your students' powers of observation and curiosity, as well. Ask them to choose any landmark on campus of interest or a few of the buildings. Often students have no idea why or for whom the buildings are named. This story is only effective if you have good archives in your campus library.

7. Online scavenger hunts

The answers to these scavenger hunts may vary according to your state, the date and the search engines or sites that students use. Access them on the book Web site at *http://info.wadsworth.com/rich*. Here are possible answers.

Online scavenger hunt #1

Weather Stories

1. Find a site that offers a list of hurricanes, and write the name of the site and the URL; then answer these questions: **Clue:** Check the National Hurricane Center. *http://www.nhc.noaa.gov/* Scroll down to historical information:

    a.   Name the costliest hurricane in the United States since 1900.
             Andrew:
    b.   When and where did it occur? 1992, Southeast Fla. and Louisiana
    c.   How much were the damages? $26.5 billion

2. Earthquakes.

    a.   *http://earthquake.usgs.gov/hazards/prepare.html*

Plane Crashes

3.   Check the National Transportation Safety Board under aviation and do a query for your state in the past year or two. *http://www.ntsb.gov/*
Go to Aviation to Accident Synopses. Access Database Query. The answers will vary according to your state and the dates you include. You might specify a year or a number of months within a year.

    a, b, and c. depend on your state.
    d. Go back to the Aviation page and click on Major Investigations: Answer: Alaska Airlines Flight 261. Pacific Ocean near Point Mugu, Calif.

U.S. Census Statistics

4. Using the most recent census, localize this story: **Clue:** U.S. Census Bureau – people – projections for your state. Start with *www.cenus.gov*. You can click on State and county Quick Facts for a fast answer. Answers depend on your state. *http://www.census.gov/population/projections/state/stpjrace.txt*

Crime Stories

5. Check the Florida Dept. of Law Enforcement Sex Offender Registry.
   > Go to *http://www.fdle.state.fl.us/*. Check sexual predators. Search the database.
   > **a.** Richard Olden Brown: He absconded. Last known address unknown.
   > **b.** Offense: rape/strongarm

6. Search the U.S. Dept. of Education's Office of Postsecondary Education for campus security statistics. *http://www.ed.gov/offices/OPE/* Go to the Resources for Institutions to A-Z index to Campus Crime to data on campus crime.

   You can also check an organization called Security on Campus. *http://campussafety.org/* Check crime stats. See how they compare with the Education Dept. site.
   Check the police statistics on your own university's Web site (if they are listed) and compare them with the ones listed on the education site.
   Answers depend on your state and university

Political Reporting

7. Check the Federal Elections Commission. *http://www.fec.gov/1996/states/aksen6.htm* to view senate campaigns by state.

8. Check *www.followthemoney.org*. Go to who's giving and who's getting. Also check *www.opensecrets.org*.

Government Statistics

9. Fedstats.gov
   a. Latest government figures for tuition costs of college and universities. (Check under fast facts for education). Go to Education to National Center for Education Statistics. Access Encyclopedia of Education Statistics to Postsecondary Education to Finances. *http://nces.ed.gov/* - to fast facts – to tuition
   (http://nces.ed.gov/fastfacts/display.asp?id=76)

   b. Average tuition, fees, room and board at four-year public institutions for the latest year available? For the 1999-2000 academic year, annual prices for undergraduate tuition, room, and board were estimated to be $7,302 at public colleges and $20,277 at private colleges.
   c. Average tuition, fees, room and board at four-year private colleges and universities? These statistics will change as figures are updated. Between 1989-90 and 1999-2000, prices at public colleges have risen by 22 percent, and prices at private colleges have increased by 27 percent, after adjustment for inflation.

10. Find the home page for your state. Write the URL.

Online scavenger hunt #2 answers

International Information

1. The U.S. Department of State issues warnings for U.S. travelers. *http://www.state.gov/*
  a. Haiti warning: American citizens should avoid all such gatherings, as crowd behavior can be unpredictable. Travelers encountering roadblocks, demonstrations, or large crowds should remain calm and depart the area quickly and without confrontation. (as of 2001)
  b. Mexico: weapons violations: Mexico has severe penalties for taking in any type of firearm, weapon, or ammunition without first obtaining written authorization from Mexican authorities.

2. Try a universal currency converter. *http://www.xe.com/ucc/*
  a. How many French francs can you get for $100 in U.S. dollars. 13.7630 (as of 2001)
  b. How many Mexican pesos will your $10 be worth? 1.10339 USD (as of 2001)

3. International time clock. *http://www.timeanddate.com/worldclock/*
There are several other possibilities.

Background Research

4. Tom French: Check the Pulitzer site: *http://www.pulitzer.org/* and read his bio. Information on his books may also be found at amazon.com. What is the name of his prize-winning series? Angels & Demons
  a. What books has he written? *A Cry in the Night*, which chronicles a murder case in Gulfport, Florida; *South of Heaven*.
  b. Where does he work? St. Petersburg Times

5. Concert review quote: Bartlett's quotations. *http://www.bartleby.com/100/*
  a. Twelfth Night.
  b. William Shakespeare

6. Bee stings. Yearbook of Experts, Authorities and Spokespersons. *http://www.yearbook.com/*
  a. Vespa Laboratories, Inc.
  b. Miles W. Guralnick, president

7. Stop-the-hate.org credibility: betterwhois.com;
  a. Site author: Steven J. Beikirch
  b. Address and telephone number: P.O. Box 3492, Bryan, TX 77805
     936-394-2600

Personal Information
8. Use mapsonus or any mapping program. mapsonus.com

9. Try Yahoo's people search or another search engine's white pages. Answers individual.

10. Site: Detroit Free Press: Freep: Jobspage
  a. *http://www.freep.com/jobspage/index.htm*
  b. How many clips does he recommend that you attach to your internship or job application? six to 10.

11. Media organizations:

    a. *www.prsa.org*

    b. *www.rtnda.org*

    c. *www.asne.org*

12. *http://www.infoplease.com/ipa/A0778562.* Answer: Norway

Workbook Exercises

6-3. Online sources

1. plagiarism.org, *http://www.plagiarism.org/*

2. *http://www.sej.org/resource/index.htm*

3. Nassau County, N.Y. Using the 2000 U.S. Census, find the following information:

    a. Percent of population change from 1990-2000: 3.6%

    b. Percent of people over 65 years old:15%

    a. Percent of black or African American persons in 2000: 10.1

4. Centers for Disease Control: Go to *www.cdc.gov/* Disease facts and information to chlamydia fact sheet in the United States:

http://www.cdc.gov/nchstp/dstd/Fact_Sheets/chlamydia_facts.htm

    a. Chlamydia is a sexually transmitted disease (STD) that is caused by the bacterium *Chlamydia trachomatis.*

    b. an estimated 3 million cases occur annually.

5. *www.yearbook.com* Alex Goldfayn, president, Strategic Consulting Group, LLC, P.O. Box 7407, Buffalo Grove, IL 60089, Phone: 847-459-6322, fax 847, 459, 8622

6. Jobs with largest growth: *http://www.bls.gov/news.release/ooh.t01.htm*

    a. food preparation and service workers

    b. customer service representatives

    c. registered nurses

(other possible answers include computer software engineers (applications), computer support specialists, and computer software engineers (systems software).

4. Go to *www.obituary.com* and click public figures.

    a. Carl Barks, creator of Donald Duck.

    b. Aug. 25, 2000; cancer.

    c. Click individuals; under H. find Hearst. Lover: Marion Davies

    d. "Citizen Kane"

4. *http://www.infoplease.com/spot/scandal2.html*

    a. illegitimate child

    b. Dean Smith, Bob Knight, Denny Crum

    http://www.infoplease.com/ipsa/A0003607.html (search for "most NCAA tournaments.")

4. *http://www.cia.gov/cia/publications/factbook/* 13.72 million sq. km of 14 million

10. The answers will vary but will give students a good idea of how to research the different cost of living indexes. Search in google.com for cost of living or salary calculators. Using virtualrelocation.com, the cost of living in San Francisco, Calif., is 174.7percent higher than that of Kansas City, Mo. A salary of $50,000 in Kansas City, Mo., has the same buying power that a salary of $137,342 has in San Francisco, Calif. (with virtual relocation) it is $127,000 in San Francisco with homefair.com.

Interviewing Techniques 7

Goals

- To teach students how to plan and conduct an interview
- To give students techniques for devising questions
- To teach students to gather information for graphics
- To teach students tips for telephone interviewing

This chapter offers many tips to help students conduct interviews, but the best way to teach students how to interview people is to let them do it. In the beginning they may not research enough background, ask enough questions or get enough sources. But the more they interview people, the more comfortable they will become. For this reason, I assign students to plan and gather information for their own stories from the beginning of the course, even before we reach this chapter.

By the time we study the interviewing skills – usually the third to fourth week into the course – students can discuss problems they are experiencing. Because the coaching method stresses helping students during the reporting and writing process and with revision afterward, the students' fears of failure are diminished. Even a bad interview is a good learning experience.

Teaching Suggestions

One of the main problems to help students overcome is "the dumb factor," their fear of appearing stupid in front of sources. Stress that they need to ask as many questions as possible to understand the issue, and it doesn't matter if some of them seem dumb. One tip that helps them lose some of their self-consciousness is what I call the "invisible factor." I tell them that the source is more interested in what he or she is saying. You (the student) are not important during the interview; you are invisible.

Another major problem students have during the interview is a lack of good follow-up questions. You can simplify the mystery of follow-up questions by asking students to think of these three: how, why and give me an example. You could also stress the key-word technique of conversational

38

questioning, discussed in the previous chapter, to give them clues about what follow-up questions to ask. The GOAL method is helpful for certain types of stories, particularly programs and profiles, but warn students that this doesn't work for all stories.

Coaching

Pair up students and have them coach each other on the story focus and questions they plan to ask for an outside assignment. This is particularly helpful for beginning students, especially before their first outside interview,

Team reporting: Pairing students to take different aspects of the same story or to do the same interview is a technique that benefits some students because they can brainstorm better and help each other during an interview. I have used this with beginning students after they have done a few interviews, rather than for their first story. I've also used it with more advanced students on issue-story assignments or major project assignments.

Taping student interviews: If you have access to videotape equipment, you can let students interview each other or you about a topic you assign. Then videotape them and let them analyze their questions and mannerisms.

Larry Campbell, one of my former colleagues at the University of Alaska Anchorage, asks students to go to a shopping mall and ask shoppers what they have purchased. It's a way to get students to approach strangers. Then they discuss who was receptive to them and who was not. The answers can be interesting.

Textbook Exercises

1. Interview a reporter

If you invite a reporter to class, distribute some of the reporter's stories before he or she plans to visit so students can ask specific questions. You may prefer to ask students to choose their own reporter and write a brief report. However, you should coordinate this so students do not interview the same reporter. You could also have students work in groups to interview a subject.

2. Icebreakers

At the beginning of class, I ask students to visit my office for a minute just to see where it is if they have not been there. Then I ask them to write five items they noticed, excluding the desk, shelves and computer. After that we discuss these items as icebreakers as though they were going to interview me.

3. Note taking

This can be fun if you play a short tape and stress that students should try to get as many good quotes as possible. Then have students read one or two quotes and compare their versions to note whether they wrote it accurately. Play the tape back so they can check their notes.

4. Notes

It is helpful to check students' notes on their outside stories to see whether they have problems getting quotes, asking good questions or just writing clearly.

5. Police officer

It may be easier to invite an officer to class so students are not ganging up on the same source. Ask the officer to discuss the type of information police may or may not provide.

6. Technical clarity

This exercise is geared more to advanced students but can be used successfully with beginners. Here is an excerpt from one student's paper explaining how a car works.

Driving down the highway at 60 miles per hour, your car suddenly stops. No power. After pulling off to the shoulder, several tow trucks swoop down like vultures. When you arrive at the garage, car doctor Leonard Orcutt tells you the dreaded news; the timing belt broke. The bill will come close to $1,500, he says. Here is how he explains it.

"The timing belt times the crankshaft to move the pistons. The valves stop when the belt breaks. But the pistons keep moving. The pistons then hit the valves, which are open. They bend. We'll have to take the head off to replace the bent valves," he said.

"Mr. Orcutt, I don't understand anything you said except for the money part," I said.

(Orcutt tries to explain. This is how the writer interprets his comment.)

The pistons and valves are involved in a fatal attraction. The dance they perform takes place very fast. Four thousand times a minute the four pistons go up and down.

When each piston goes down, the valve above it opens and sucks in gas. As the piston rises again, the valve closes. When the piston is near the top, the compressed gas combines with sparks from a spark plug to create a miniature explosion. The burnt gases are forced out of the cylinder.

The one piece of equipment that synchronizes this dance between the pistons and the valves is the timing belt. Orcutt held up a used timing belt, a flat piece of black rubber with rubber teeth. The teeth fit perfectly into the grooves of the crankshaft and camshaft. The belt ran both shafts like one heart for two Siamese twins.

Lee Hill. Reprinted with permission.

7. Graphics

This exercise reinforces the need to ask questions that will provide information for graphics. Whenever possible, remind students to think graphically.

8. Enterprise story

By now students should be developing their own stories and getting practice in interviewing. These suggestions are rather ordinary, and I would encourage students to get better ones. However, because many students have such trouble finding story ideas, these can be used as a starting point.

Workbook Exercises

7-1 to 7-3. Listening, interviewing, concentration.

The listening and concentration exercises are intended to make students aware of their listening skills. They are not scientific, but students may enjoy the self-examination. The interviewing exercise is another chance for students to take notes and ask questions.

7-4. Coaching

It would be ideal if you had time to coach all students before they wrote stories, but few teachers have that much time. Although peer coaching is not as effective, it helps students to discuss their stories with anyone before they write. If you use class time for this, you can walk around and spot problems or coach some students who need your help. You can also follow this activity with a class discussion of common problems the students experienced.

7-5. Observing interviewing techniques

Place students in groups of three. One person will be the observer and the other two will interview each other; then rotate. Suggest any topic about which they can interview each other – tuition or fee increases, tips for coping with stress, pros and cons of living with a roommate or loved one, or a reaction to a local or national story. Have the observer fill out the form. Then have the groups discuss the strengths and weaknesses they noticed in their classmates' interviewing techniques.

7-6. E-mail interview

My students have had mixed reactions to e-mail interviewing. The shy ones really like it. I have found e-mail interviews very unsatisfactory unless the questions are limited. However, it is worth trying, especially if students only need a brief answer. People may be more accessible by e-mail, but this form of interviewing prevents follow-up questions and does not provide visual clues for observation of details and other techniques that enhance writing.

7-7. Interview a news source

This exercise comes from my former colleague, Mary Wallace, assistant dean at the University of Kansas journalism school. Wallace asks students to interview a source who has been in the news or who deals with the media frequently. Students should find out what good or bad experiences the source has had with the media. Let students recommend which sources they want to interview, but you will need to check and make sure there are no duplications. It also helps to tell sources that their comments will only be used in a report for class, not for publication; otherwise you will not get much candor. Some suggested sources include any public information officer, city officials, university administrators frequently in the news, athletes, coaches, sports information directors, a police information officer or the police chief.

7-8. Beyond the 5 W's

This exercise is adapted from Donald M. Murray, a retired English professor from the University of New Hampshire, who is considered the founder of the coaching movement. It can help students ask follow-up questions and probe beyond the basics. This exercise also lends itself to group brainstorming. You could place the students in small groups and then write some of their answers on the board or discuss other questions these basic ones generate.

7-9. Dissect a newspaper story

Use the same story in class so students can compare their questions. You can use a campus or local newspaper or access an online story so students are all working on the same article.

The Writing Process   8

Goals

- To help students develop a writing process
- To teach students the importance of revision
- To teach students how to plan a nonlinear story for the Web
- To teach the AP style for the following: titles, pounds, numbers (cardinal and ordinal), seasons, trademarks (Dumpster), quotation mark punctuation, it's/its, T-shirt, age, and time in the workbook style test.

Teaching Suggestions

If you ask students and professional writers where they struggle when they write their stories, the most common answers are leads and organization. By teaching students how to develop good habits in the writing process, you can help them avoid some of the pitfalls of suffering over leads and organization. Coaching tips that help many writers are:

- Free-write a first draft.
- Write many leads instead of suffering until you get the perfect one.
- Spend a few minutes jotting down a rough order for your story before you begin writing.

Although students often say they have the order for their story in their minds, encourage them to write a brief plan; it forces them to think. It also helps to remind students to write a focus sentence on top of their stories.

Training students to write briefs that summarize the story for the Web and plan nonlinear Web stories will reinforce the concept of focus and prepare them to think critically about how Web stories differ from print.

If you teach the FORK method, warn students not to overuse the repetition of key words. Although you may object to the slang term "kiss off," I have found that students remember better than just telling them to block information.

If your students are struggling with organization of their stories, ask them to attach their rough outline when they submit their stories or their notes to help you identify whether their problems are due to reporting, note taking, poor planning or writing.

Textbook Exercises

1. Write a plan for organizing a story

Although this activity is intended to be used with outside assignments, you can ask students to do this with a class assignment as well. It helps students to get in the habit of drafting a rough plan before they write.

2. Free-writing

This is an exercise for students who struggle organizing their stories. Ask students to write a rough draft from what they remember without looking at their notes. Then they can check their notes for quotes and facts. For some writers, it helps to get thoughts on paper, no matter how disorganized they are. Then the writers can look at their rough draft and begin forming a plan to organize it.

3. Revision

If you have stories in your local or campus newspaper that are not clearly written, pull one and distribute it to the class or ask students to find one. Meeting stories often lend themselves to this exercise. Profiles and features also may have extraneous quotes and transitions. If students have written a full-length story, they could revise their own stories.

4. FORK exercise

This exercise is geared to beginning students, although it works for advanced students as well. It reinforces the idea of blocking sources in one place (the "kiss-off" technique). Warn students to avoid stringing quotes together. No one order is correct. The focus of this story is the resurgence of blind dates in New York City. Here is the original story if you want to distribute it to students:

Blind dates are back, romance experts say

NEW YORK – It was a blind date. They decided to meet by the Dumpster in front of Jeremy's Ale House, a popular hangout at Manhattan's South Street Seaport. Expectations were low.

Barbara Wasserman had been turned off when, on the telephone, her date said he would be the good-looking guy in the blue suit. And Bob Goldman had already slogged through five blind dates, all of them letdowns.

"I found the Dumpster, put down my briefcase and saw a sea of blue suits," Wasserman recalled. "All of a sudden a truly good-looking guy in a blue suit came out of the crowd, smiling, and kissed me on the cheek."

That night, the two shared a pitcher of beer, walked to Chinatown, spoke in French, ate dinner and discussed work, drinking games, politics, travel, mutual friends and college experiences. Fourteen months later, in the fall of 1986, a marriage proposal came in the form of a diamond ring tucked inside a fortune cookie. Theirs was, admittedly, an unusual ending to what has become a fairly common prelude to romance in New York City: the blind date.

With bars and nightclubs considered unacceptable meeting grounds by many in the era of AIDS, more men and women are depending on their friends to match them with others whose sexual histories, interest and looks are, at least to some extent, known entities.

"Someone you trust says there's this guy who's really great," said Pamela Harris, a 26-year-old associate art director. "There's a sense of safety. You feel like you're not being thrown to the wolves. A friend has insight into me and knows the kind of men I like, so basically, she's just cropped out 80 percent of the male population."

Steven Veer, 28, a Manhattan attorney, who has been on dozens of blind dates, said: "Personals are a last resort. A blind date is much better. It's a screen. You know the person hasn't 'over-circulated' in this time of caution. . . ."

The "set-up" or "fix-up," as it is often called, has hit other parts of the nation as well.

"In law school my friends and I live on blind dates," said Morris Panner, 25, now in his last semester at Harvard. "Five years ago, I would have thought it was really crass."

New Yorkers, however, seem to have an especially urgent need for blind dates. "New York can be a really lonely place," said Melissa Mack, 24, who works in public relations.

"Everyone acquires an anonymous character. On the subway, the same people kicking and shoving and ignoring you might be loving and caring in a relationship."

And clubs often can seem as alienating as the subway. "What's so disenchanting about the club scene is that being cool and detached is the order of the day," Mack said.

What's left, then, is a vestige of an earlier period in America's social history.

"Not long ago, a person willing to go on a blind date was perceived as a poor nebbish who had to rely on someone else to meet people," said Dr. Herbert J. Freudenberger, a New York City psychologist. "There's a complete shift in attitude now. It's a subtle swing back to a more conservative time."

Authorities in the field of romance have also noted the trend toward blind dating. It's happening, absolutely, said Sharon Lependorf, a consultant at People Resources, a New York singles club. "I've had at least three friends who got married in the last year and a half who met on blind dates."

Dr. Nathaniel Brandon, a Los Angeles psychologist and the author of "The Psychology of Romantic Love" and "How to Raise Your Self-Esteem," both published by Bantam, said, "Today, when people find it so hard to meet other people and when there is so much fear of different diseases, it's predictable and inevitable that we could see a resurgence of blind dating."

Amy Jaffe is a master matchmaker. "There's a Jewish legend," she said, "that if you fix up two people and they get married and have children, you're guaranteed a place in heaven. I have three marriages under my belt, so I guess I'm in good shape."

What is her secret? "Usually, people try to fix others up on the basis that they both like to ski or they both like Islamic art," said Jaffe, a 29-year-old journalist. "But I find those things don't make a difference. Instead, I ask friends to describe the last person they were in love with."

Lisa W. Foderaro, *The New York Times*. Reprinted with permission.

5. Web story

Teach students how to think in nonlinear fashion for the Web. They can use the previous story or any story in their campus or local newspapers. Ask them to plan links and interactive elements such as a poll or quiz.

Workbook Exercises

8-1. FORK exercise

This FORK exercise is a little harder than the one in the textbook and is offered here to give you a choice of assignments, especially if you have an advanced class. This story offers the possibility of a simple focus that college freshmen often gain 15 pounds – indicated in the nut graph, the third paragraph. Or students could focus on the fact that researchers believe the "Freshman 15" is a myth, in which case they would have to organize the story with backup to this focus higher in the story. The sources can be in almost any order.

You could add reporting skills to this story by encouraging students to interview other students or check Web sites about this subject. Here is the original story for comparative purposes.

The freshman food fight

Pizza and philosophy at midnight. Cheese fries and chitchat at 2 a.m. Psychology and popcorn for breakfast.

That's college life, where sleep is cheap, calories abound and freshman math is as easy as counting to 15 – the Freshman 15.

Those nasty 10 to 15 pounds that students tend to gain in the first few months of college have become as much a part of higher education as reading lists and blue-book exams.

The Freshman 15 has been the topic of academic studies, nutritionists' newsletters and just plain talk among the college crowd.

"I think I've already gained it," said Vanessa Varvarezis, who has been a freshman at Villanova University for three weeks.

"My parents sent me away with four bags of junk food, and it's almost half gone already," said Varvarezis, a tall woman with a broad smile and thin hips.

Eating at Donahue Hall one recent evening, Varvarezis had spaghetti, garlic bread, vegetables, about eight cookies and a fudge ice-cream pop.

"It was Weight Watchers, though," she said.

According to a calorie chart given out by Villanova food-services staff, Varvarezis had eaten more than 900 calories for dinner. And that was before the late-night pizza run.

"I order out a lot," Varvarezis said. "Grease, grease, lots of grease."

Some schools, such as the University of Pennsylvania and Rutgers University, offer special workshops to freshman students to help them avoid the weight gain.

Often, students eat out of stress and even more often in an effort to socialize and fit in, said Peg Abell, a nutritionist at Widener University.

"Some people eat to feel better since eating can have a soothing effect, and some use eating as a way of maintaining control of at least one portion of their life," she said.

The fabled Freshman 15 affects men and women, according to students.

"I've gained 20 pounds since I left home," said Gene Lamm, a junior at Beaver cake with two friends.

Lifting his gray T-shirt, Lam chuckled and said: "I used to have abs (abdominal muscles); I don't know what happened to them."

Some men said they welcomed the extra weight gain.

"I went up for second portions every day," said Joe Leung, a junior at Villanova. "I weighed 115 when I came, and I got up to 140."

Despite the endless stories from students, some researchers claim the Freshman 15 is just a bunch of bunk.

"A myth," said Stephen Bailey, a sociology professor who conducted a weight-gain study for Tufts University in Massachusetts.

Bailey and Tufts nutrition professor Jeanne Goldberg tracked 120 women through their first year of college.

"Basically, we came up with some results that surprised us," Bailey said. "On average, the women gained a little bit less than a pound. They gained a bit between the fall and spring and lost all of that over the course of the summer." Bailey said the participants in the study were volunteers.

Don't spout off any of those statistical findings to Missy Palko, a sophomore at Beaver College. She, like scores of others, can shoot down the conclusion with personal experience.

"I gained 30 pounds last year," she said. "If you look in the closets around here, they're all packed with food."

An informal survey of dorm residents proved her right. Room after room held stashes of cheese crackers, doughnuts, popcorn, frosted breakfast cereals, chocolate and sodas.

And then there was pizza. Delivered.

"We call them the pie hours," said Jim Martin, manager of California Style Pizza. From 9 p.m. to 2 a.m. he said, his six employees, deliver up to 50 pizzas per hour to the nearby campus.

And once that smell of melted cheese and thick sauce fills the dorm halls, Martin said, his delivery people have no problem "hawking pizzas." He routinely makes four extra pizzas for them to take along and sell on the spot. It never fails.

Nutritionists agree it's understandable that students who stay up late to study need to eat to keep going. The nutritionists' newsletters suggest that fruit or even pretzels would be healthier snacks than candy or pizza.

Weight gain doesn't frighten Craig Zabransky, a Villanova freshman, eating dinner at Donahue Hall.

"Well I'm not having nightmares about it," he said, as he dug into a generous spaghetti dinner and his fourth piece of buttery garlic bread. "I'm just going to exercise more. I'm going to start tomorrow."

Tanya Barrientos, *The Philadelphia Inquirer*. Reprinted with permission.

47

8-2. Revision to tighten and correct style

The style corrections and words that should be eliminated are crossed out in boldface type within parentheses. A copy of the original story also follows so you can see it more clearly without the redundancies.

(A woman named) Shirley Anne Hall has (up) until December 8 (Dec. 8) to clear (up) her Garden Grove house of rotten oranges (that have gone bad), cobwebs, vehicle parts, musty newspapers and a year's worth of dirty dishes (that have not been washed).

Hall, (who is age) 54, must remove overgrown weeds (in her yard) and other debris from her yard (which is located) in the 12,000 (12000 is correct style; eliminate comma after 12) block of Barlett Street, Orange County, (S)uperior (C)ourt (J)udge Randell Wilkinson said (on) Wednsday (Wednesday). If she fails to comply, (with the order which judge Randell Wilkinson made on Wednesday) the city will bring in work crews and send Hall the bill (for the work the crews have done).

The city has been trying to persuade Hall to sort through her mess since (the year of) 1988, (C)ity (A)ttorney Stuart Scudder said.

Hall, (a woman) who is diagnosed with chronic depression, said the city is harrassing (harassing) her and (that) the stress (that the city has caused her by harrassing her) has prevented her from making any progress.

The Dayle McIntosh Center for the Disabled in Anaheim is looking for volunteers (who of their own volition will offer) to help Hall to clean up.

Here is the original story:

Shirley Anne Hall has until Dec. 8 to clear her Garden Grove home of rotten oranges, cobwebs, vehicle, parts, musty newspapers and a year's worth of dirty dishes.

Hall, 54, also must remove overgrown weeds and other debris from her yard in the 12000 block of Bartlett Street, Orange County Superior Court Judge Randell Wilkinson said Wednesday. If she fails to comply, the city will bring in work crews and send Hall the bill.

The city has been trying to persuade Hall to sort through her mess since 1988, City Attorney Stuart Scudder said.

Hall, diagnosed with chronic depression, said the city is harassing her and the stress has prevented her from making any progress.

The Dayle McIntosh Center for the Disabled in Anaheim is looking for volunteers to help Hall clean up.

The Orange County (Calif.) *Register.* Reprinted with permission.

8-3. Style Test

Here are suggested corrections:

1. Fourteen months later in the fall of 1986, Bob Goldman proposed marriage by tucking a diamond ring inside a fortune cookie.

2. Barbara Wasserman and Bob Goldman had low expectations that their blind date would work out.

3. Christopher Carter, an officer in a public relations firm, gave a speech.

4. Police arrested a 24-year-old man last night and charged him with possession of an illegal substance.

5. Two university professors conducted a survey of students to determine weight gain among college freshmen.

Corrections for these sentences are in boldface type in parentheses.

6. Stephen Bailey, a Sociology **(sociology)** professor, says the idea that freshmen gain fifteen lbs. **(15 pounds)** is "a myth". **(myth." - period inside quote marks)**.

7. Women gained a little bit less than 1 **(1 is correct; figures for weights)** pound, between Fall **(fall)** and Spring **(spring)** but they lost it during the Summer **(summer; lowercase for seasons)**.

8. Barbara Wasserman met her future fiance by the dumpster **(Dumpster is a trademark)**.

9. She said its **(it's)** a good thing that she decided to go on the blind date.

10. Lamm lifted his tee-shirt **(T-shirt)** to reveal his expanding stomach.

11. Amy Jaffee, a 29-year-old journalist, says most romances that are arranged fizzle after the 2nd or 3rd **(second or third)** date.

12. From 9 P.M. to 2 A.M. **(9 p.m. to 2 a.m.)** Jim Martin delivers up to fifty **(50)** pizzas to Villanova University students.

13. 120 **(One hundred twenty)** women were surveyed for the weight-gain study.

14. Nathaniel Branden said, "Its **(It's)** predictable and inevitable that we would see a resurgence of blind dating". **(." period inside quotes)**.

15. Gene Lamm said he gained twenty lbs. **(20 pounds)** during his freshman year of college.

Leads and Nut Graphs

9

Goals

- To teach students how to write hard-news leads, second-day leads and impact leads
- To teach students how to use delayed identification
- To explain active and passive voice
- To teach students how to use attribution in leads
- To teach students how to write soft leads and nut graphs
- To test students for the Associated Press style concepts in the following: numbers, age, percents, times, money, addresses, dimensions, dates, punctuation inside quotations, vote counts, hyphens.

This chapter is geared to beginning and advanced students. For beginners, you may want to stress hard-news leads and impact leads at first, but they should also learn how to write soft leads so they can experience the creative aspects of newswriting. For advanced students, the hard-news leads can serve as a refresher, and more emphasis can be placed on teaching soft leads, which may be new to them. The textbook exercises offer students a chance to practice writing some leads in class, and the workbook offers more lead-writing exercises. This is an important chapter for skill development, and it may take a few class periods to teach.

Teaching Suggestions

Many students and professional writers struggle with leads, so the coaching tips are particularly important. Two of the most helpful tips are to write several leads for a story or to start with the nut graph instead of struggling over the perfect lead.

When teaching summary leads, emphasize that students do not have to put all the five W's in the lead. Also stress that their leads must be backed up with supporting information. Help them understand that if they can't back up the lead, they have the wrong lead.

Students also have difficulty understanding how anecdotal, narrative and descriptive leads differ. In many cases, leads combine all these types of writing; the terms are not important. But if they study the examples, students can distinguish some differences in writing styles.

Many instructors prefer to teach leads at the beginning of the course. If you prefer that order, this chapter is self-contained enough for you to use at any point in your course. The writing techniques can serve as inspiration for the reporting process, particularly for soft leads. Stress that students cannot write soft leads if they don't gather the right information, such as description and anecdotes, during the reporting process.

Textbook Exercises

1. Hard-news leads

These exercises should test students' ability to emphasize the main point.

a. This lead should stress the reason students switch majors as in these examples:

Poor teaching and an aloof faculty were cited as the main causes 60 percent of engineering and mathematics students switch majors in college, according to a study released Monday by the University of Colorado.

or

Sixty percent of college students who begin studying science, mathematics or engineering switch majors, according to a study released Monday by the University of Colorado.

b. This lead should stress the injuries to the firefighters and/or the damages to the restaurant, such as this lead:

Two firefighters were injured in a fire at a pizza restaurant at 2035 Main Street when the roof collapsed.

or

A fire at a pizza restaurant at 2035 Main St. caused an estimated $100,000 in damages and injured two firefighters when the roof collapsed.

c. This lead should stress what the survey said. Tell students to avoid general leads such as *The Centers for Disease Control released a survey.* Also warn them to be careful and note that the proper title is Centers, not Center. Here are some students' leads:

Many vitamins, protein supplements and muscle growth products have no medical support for their advertised claims, according to a survey released today by the Centers for Disease Control.

*　　　*　　　*

Nutritional supplements often don't live up to their advertised claims and have "no documented medical effect," according to a study released today by the Centers for Disease Control.

2. Active/passive voice

a. Active: A 29-year-old Phoenix man died Tuesday when his motorcycle was struck by a car on East Ina Road.

b. Passive: A 17-year-old high school sophomore was sentenced yesterday to two consecutive life terms for the murder of two men in a convenience store.

3. Delayed identification

The man's age or city may be used as an identifier, but both are better.

A 44-year old Tucson man was killed yesterday when he lost control of his truck and was thrown from the vehicle on East 15th Street near South Kino Parkway, police said.
Michael Stephens, of the 3700 block of North Camino Street, died of head injuries at the scene of the accident at 2:30 a.m.

4. Updated lead

Stress what will happen today.

Classes at Midtown Magnet Middle School will resume today.
School was closed yesterday while employees cleaned up damage from vandals who broke into the school on Sunday.

5. Impact leads

Students may use second-person voice "you" or the noun in these leads to focus on who is affected by the action.
a. Students who live in residence halls at (name of University) will pay as much as 14.8 percent more for a double room next fall.

b. Owners of electronic security systems could be paying a $30 penalty every time their security systems set off a false alarm, if the Rockville City Council passes an ordinance setting penalties at Tuesday's meeting.

6. Attribution

If students use the cause of the fire, and they should, this lead should be attributed because the cause of the fire is an informed opinion or a fact that is not general knowledge.

Soft leads

These leads can vary considerably but most start with a specific example and proceed to the general nut graph; here are some examples.

7. Anecdotal focus-on-a-person lead

This should start with Nancy Pauw, either using her name or referring to her with delayed identification.

After circling the parking lot east of the computer center three times, Nancy Pauw finally found a space.

"I have to get here an hour early so I can get to class on time," said Pauw, a graduate student at the University of . . . .

Pauw is one of many (substitute your university) students who experience the daily frustration of not finding parking spaces even though they have purchased the $30 and $50 permits.

Christine Laue, *The University Daily Kansan.* Reprinted with permission.

8. Specific to general

A vacuum cleaner is worth $800,000, a dishwasher is worth $700,000 and a fire engine is worth only one cent. Those are the estimates of property in the National Park Service records.

A report issued yesterday by the General Accounting Office claims the Park service financial statements are inaccurate and filled with accounting errors.

9. Descriptive lead

Duct tape keeps the banister in place on the stairs leading to the attic apartment at 1032 Main St. The kitchen is infested with mice and roaches. The bathroom has no electricity.

"It's a dump," said Flis, a senior majoring in architecture. "But it was the cheapest thing I could find."

The stories are similar for many students at the University of Kansas. They live in Oread neighborhood apartments that are considered hazardous by Lawrence city officials.

David Silverman, *The University Daily Kansan.* Reprinted with permission.

10. Narrative lead

This could start with the third paragraph as indicated:

Louis Cortez spotted a man walking toward the ledge on the roof of the garage at St. Francis Hospital about 8:40 a.m. Sunday. Cortez, a public safety officer, stopped his vehicle and told the man to move away from the ledge.

The man shook his head "No."

"I stepped out and asked him, 'Can I help you sir?' and he said, 'I'm going to jump,'" Cortez said.

The man was a 36-year-old patient from Topeka State Hospital (continue with story).

11. Leads analysis

This exercise is more time consuming than it seems, and you should warn students that it may take them a few hours. My students have always found this very helpful. I think it encourages students to read the newspaper critically and to begin reading for writing techniques as well as content. I used to ask students to type the leads they chose because I thought it would make them more conscious of the writing, but it saves time if they just clip them and attach them to their papers. For class discussion I ask students to read a few of the leads they chose. Invariably, a lead one student chose as an excellent example is one another student chose for the leads he or she disliked. This can prompt a good class discussion about how differently people react to stories and writing styles.

12. Web leads

This exercise is intended to reinforce to students that Web leads must have the main point in the lead or high in the story because Web readers have too many other choices and want information quickly. Some possibilities:

a. Alcohol-related arrests on college campuses surged 24.3 percent last year, according to a survey released today.

b. Rats dream, too. Researchers are studying the rodents' dreams to find out how human brains work.

c. Your cell phone won't give your cancer. That's the finding of a study published this week.

Workbook Exercises

These exercises will give students much more practice writing leads. Students probably can complete fewer than 10 leads in a class period. You may want to pick only a few or have them write the rest for homework. In many cases, students' leads will be better than the leads on the original stories.

9-1. Hard-news (summary) leads

These leads should focus on the most important point. It may help students if you tell them that a summary lead is usually the same as the focus sentence.

Here are some examples from students and from the original stories:

1. Three to four children die every day from child abuse or neglect in the United States, according to a survey released yesterday.

2. Nearly 150 abortion protesters were arrested yesterday as they tried to block access to an abortion clinic during the third day of a planned six-week protest.

3. A delivery driver for a Chinese restaurant was robbed at gunpoint of the food he was delivering Monday at an apartment complex at 718 S.W. Western Ave.

4. A fire started by a lighted cigarette on a sofa caused $45,000 in damages to a two-bedroom home in the 2300 block of Main Street, officials said.

5. Murders in (your state) increased 53 percent, but the number of rapes and robberies declined during the first three months of this year, according to a report from the state Bureau of Investigation.

6. Damage to the earth's ozone layer could increase by 3 percent, leading to an increase in skin cancer during the next decade, researchers from a United Nations scientific panel reported yesterday.

7. A woman doused her wheelchair-bound husband with rubbing alcohol and set him on fire because he ate her chocolate Easter bunny, police said yesterday.
(Make sure students attribute the last one.)

9-2. Delayed identification leads

Students generally grasp the concept of delayed identification, but they need to be reminded to name the person (when applicable) in the next paragraph. You may find it helpful to have them write the first two graphs instead of just the lead. Here are some examples of leads:

1. The tears of a 13-year-old boy may have saved him his Chicago Bulls jacket Friday.

2. A founder of the American Indian Movement said yesterday that using Indians as mascots in sports promotes racism.

3. An Emporia man is in critical condition after being diagnosed with Legionnaires' disease, which state health officials suspect he contracted at an Emporia high school reunion.

4. A man wearing a white sack over his face unsuccessfully tried to rob an eastside grocery store last night.

5. A former (your town) animal control officer was arrested after authorities found 67 dead cats in her refrigerator and freezer.

9-3. Second-day leads

Explain to students that most of the time they are writing for the next morning's edition, so anything that happened today should be referred to as yesterday. However, AP style says to use the name of the day instead of "yesterday." If they are writing for an afternoon paper, they can use today. If they have a good second-day lead, they may not need the past time element in the lead at all. Concentrate on the future or next step, and put the past time element of the news in the second paragraph.

1. Beginning with next year's freshmen class, all undergraduates at (your school) will be required to take a course in cultural diversity.

2. A 43-year-old (use your town) man is in fair condition today at (hospital name) after being stabbed at a convenience store last night.

3. A 24-year-old Fairbanks man is in critical condition in a Fairbanks hospital today after he was shot by a state trooper in an early morning incident.

4. A 15-year-old Santana High School freshman will be arraigned as an adult in San Diego Superior Court Wednesday on murder charges in connection with the shooting deaths of two students and injuries to 13 people Monday.

5. A woman is in custody today while authorities try to determine how her carry-on bag contained a fake grenade used for a security screener that rolled down the aisle of an American Airlines flight Sunday.

9-4. Impact leads

1. Homeowners whose roofs were damaged during the recent hurricane have five more days to apply for free repairs provided by the U.S. Army Corps of Engineers.

2. Everyone in Topeka with a gravel driveway would be forced to park in the street if an ordinance under consideration is adopted by the Topeka City Council.

3. Full-time students at all four of the University of Missouri's campuses will pay about $240 more in tuition next year because of a new rate approved by the Missouri Board of Curators.

4. Passengers on the Massachusetts Bay Transportation subway system will be getting "smart cards" to use in an automated fare collection system.

5. Your next common cold might not last as long, thanks to a new drug that eases symptoms.

9-5. Attribution in leads

1. No attribution needed. Factual.
2. No. Factual.
3. Yes. Cause is someone's opinion, probably a fire official.
4. Yes. Accusatory; need police to give motive and accusations.
5. No. She has been charged with the crime; it is public record.
6. Yes. Accusation.

9-6. Soft leads

Students usually enjoy expressing their creativity in soft leads. Warn them not to make up any information and to pull the lead from something in the story. The first lead especially encourages them to have fun. Some examples:

1. Soft lead using any technique
(Students' versions:)

A Topeka police officer was all shook up and a Topeka resident was left doing the jailhouse rock yesterday because of Elvis.

•   •   •

Elvis was in the middle of a domestic fight yesterday.

•   •   •

Most Elvis sightings are unusual, but Officer Chuck Haggard saw the King flying at him Wednesday.

2. Focus on a person

Four years ago, Tamera Podwolsky answered phones eight hours a day.

But things change.

Today Podwolsky, 35, straps on a tool belt and a hard hat and heads for work at local construction sites as a carpentry apprentice.

She is one of more than 4,000 single parents and displaced homemakers who have received vocational training, education and job placement from Project for Homemakers in Arizona Seeking Employment – PHASE.

Adapted from a story by Angelica Pence, *The Arizona Daily Star.*

3. Descriptive "show-in-action" lead

Robert Thompson stood on his newly repaired front porch and watched as volunteers, with tools and paintbrushes, scurried around the East Topeka neighborhood.

Thompson and his wife, Flora, were unable to pay for repairs to their home after a van hit the side of their house more than a year ago. Matters became worse when Johnson suffered a stroke that left her paralyzed on her left side.

But Saturday good fortune knocked on their door in the form of Model Block 1992, a home renovation program for homeowners who are elderly or disadvantaged and unable to repair their homes.

Thompson was one of 45 homeowners in three Topeka neighborhoods who received the free home remodeling as part of that program.

Sandra Moran, *The Topeka Capital-Journal.* Reprinted with permission

4. Narrative lead

It was a quiet Sunday morning when 19-year-old Pvt. Earl Schaeffer sat at the switchboard at Hickam Field in Oahu, Hawaii.

Not a single phone call came across the wire. The only sound was the voice on the radio, speaking during the "Lutheran Hour."

As Schaeffer sat studying a book on aerial navigation – he wanted to be a fighter pilot – he began to hear the sounds of bombing.

It hardly drew his attention; practice maneuvers were common around the base.

But the noises grew louder and louder.

"I ran out of the hangar, and I saw aircraft swooping down and dropping black objects, and it still didn't dawn on me, because I wasn't expecting anything like that."

Then he saw the large red circles painted on the sides of the planes – the symbol of Japanese fighter planes.

The date was Dec. 7, 1941.

On that day, Japanese fighter pilots bombed Pearl Harbor, Hawaii, killing 2,471 Americans and drawing the United States into World War II. The Japanese lost 55 men.

Schaeffer, now 67, is a member of the Pearl Harbor Survivors Association, a national organization with about 115 members in Kansas.

Lillian Zier, *The Salina* (Kan.) *Journal.* Reprinted with permission.

5. Mystery teaser lead

To Delores Sampson, Marriaha is "like any other kitten." She's always trying to jump up on Sampson's lap, and until recently she made a habit of sleeping on Sampson's bed.

There is, however, one big difference between Marriaha and other 22-month-old cats. Emphasis on *big.*

Marriaha is a 300-pound Bengal tiger.

Marriaha made a reputation for herself in December when she escaped from a cage on the back porch and traipsed around her front lawn, separated from the neighbor's property by just a 4-foot high chain-link fence . . . .

At the urging of neighbors, the county commissioners voted 2-1 Tuesday to pass an ordinance banning the sale or ownership of 16 species of animals "not normally domesticated."

Michael Quinlan, *The* (Louisville, Ky.) *Courier-Journal.* Reprinted with permission.

9-7. Summary and soft leads

The hard-news leads can mirror the first sentences in the exercises. Students can be creative with soft leads. Some examples:

1. A student at a Vermont private school presented the naked truth in her graduation speech. To the dismay of school officials, she disrobed in the middle of her speech.

2. For 41 years he was known as the "boy in the box." The young murder victim has been buried in a pauper's grave. But with modern technology, police plan to exhume his body and extract DNA from his remains to attempt to solve his murder.

3. Tara Reynold isn't happy about buying textbooks bundled with supplemental materials such as CD-ROMs. She is one of many students who can't resell their textbooks because of a growing process called "bundling," a method of packaging supplements with the texts.

Reynold says the supplements aren't necessary. "The teachers don't encourage or enforce their use," she says.

4. You won't need to buy a tuxedo or wedding dress if you plan to get married this Valentine's Day at a hotel in Runaway Bay, Jamaica. And you won't need sunblock. The Superclubs' Hedonism II Resort is offering a nude wedding package, complete with a minister, marriage license, cake and music.

5. Pet owners who worry about getting germs from their pets have a new concern: They can spread germs to their pets as well. A new study documents that 16 cases of staph infections in horses, cats and dogs were believed to have been spread by their owners or veterinarians.

9-8. Style quiz corrections

Corrections are in boldface type.

1. The survey shows that 3 to 4 **(three to four)** children die every day from child abuse; more than half of those who died were under age one **(1)** and seventy-nine % **(79 percent)** of the deaths were among children under age five **(5)**.

2. A fire started at 3:00 p.m. **(3 p.m.)** and caused 45 thousand dollars **($45,000)** worth of damage to a home in the 2,300 **(2300)** block of Main St. **(Street).**

3. Murders in the state are up 53% **(53 percent)** and violent crime increased two % **(2 percent).**

4. A man who threw a two-by-three foot **(2- by 3-foot)** velvet painting of Elvis Presley at officers was 42-years-old **(42 years old).**

5. Almost 2500 **(2,500)** Americans were killed at Pearl Harbor on December 7, 1941 **(Dec. 7, 1941).**

6. Tuition will increase twelve % **(12 percent)** at the University of Missouri and will effect **(affect)** students at all four campuses.

7. 45 **(Forty-five)** people volunteered to repair homes for disadvantaged people.

8. The 36 year old **(36-year-old)** patient said, "I'm going to jump". **(jump.")**

9. The two to one **(2–1)** vote by the county commission **(should be County Commission if referring to a specific commission)** to ban nondomesticated pets will effect **(affect)** Marriaha, a 300 pound **(300-pound)** Bengal tiger. (Although students may be tempted to hyphenate "nondomesticated," the word is correct in the exercise; it does not need a hyphen.)

10. The tiger lives in a house that has a four-foot **(4-foot)** fence in the front yard.

Story Structure

10

Goals

- To teach students pacing and rhythm
- To teach students techniques for endings
- To help students visualize story shapes
- To help students plan the structure of stories
- To teach the following style concepts: no capital letters for directions, apostrophes for grades and omissions before a decade ('90s) but not after, titles, "drunken" as adjective, affect/effect, ages, caliber pistol, comma after city and states in sentences.

Teaching Suggestions

To help students understand the concepts of pacing and parallelism, ask them to read stories aloud. Students will understand rhythm of words better when they hear them.

You might also ask them to bring in tapes of their favorite musical entertainers, particularly rap music or other kinds of music the students like. Let them play the tapes and analyze the rhythm. Then let them read aloud a story or excerpt and discuss whether the story also has a rhythm. You can choose some of the examples in the text or in this manual. Bad examples of cumbersome stories are equally effective in pointing out the need for rhythm in writing.

This chapter includes all these story structures in one place for convenience as a way of organizing the book. However, I prefer to teach the structures as the need arises when I introduce basic stories and features as well as stories in Part 5, Applying the Techniques. For example, the inverted pyramid and *The Wall Street Journal* formula can be introduced with a lesson on leads or storytelling and feature techniques. The hourglass form is well suited to use with crime stories and the list technique works well with material on governmental and statistical stories in Chapter 21. If you are assigning students to do an in-depth story, particularly in advanced courses, the sections technique can be taught at that time. Regardless of the form, it is important to reinforce the concept of organizing a story first by topics with one point leading logically to the next.

Textbook Exercises

1. Inverted Pyramid

MERIDEN, Conn. – The Connecticut State Police has banned the use of hand-held radar guns because of concerns troopers could develop cancer from long-term exposure to the radiation waves emitted by the devices.

The move, believed to be the first of its kind by a state police agency, comes two months after three municipal police officers filed workers' compensation claims saying they developed cancer from using hand-held radar guns.

The ban was ordered Tuesday as a precaution while studies are conducted into the possible links between cancer and use of the devices, said Adam Berluti, a state police spokesman.

"The feeling here is to err on the side of caution until more is known about the issue," Berluti said. "The whole situation is still under review."

Berluti said the ban, which withdraws 70 radar guns from service, will not affect speed enforcement. State troopers will continue to use units with transmitters mounted on the outside of cruisers, Berluti said.

The Associated Press. Reprinted with permission.

2. *The Wall Street Journal* formula

This story could have been written several ways. Any of the college sources could work for an anecdotal lead, followed by a nut graph that explains the concept of rising volunteerism. Backup for the nut graph should be relatively high in the story. The order of the anecdotal material is flexible. The original story was very long; here are some excerpts:

College students are most susceptible to online obsession, experts say

In 1995, Stacie Kawaguchi started tinkering with the Internet.

She clicked her mouse, surfed around and delved into an international pen-pal site. At the time a Kansas University graduate student in botany, Kawaguchi "met" folks from Canada, France, Japan and Brazil.

Through the Internet, she even met her eventual fiancé, a Ph.D. candidate in engineering at Virginia Tech University.

When you first start, you get really into it," said Kawaguchi, 26, now an assistant specialist in the KU Herbarium on West Campus. "You get stuck on it for long periods of time."

Simply put, Kawaguchi was online and overwhelmed.

"You stay up late instead of going to sleep," she said. "It sucked up a lot of time."

In a few months, the novelty began to wear off.

"After a while, it was like, geez, this is enough," she said, adding that many of her chat mates were there night after night, even when she was gone for weeks at a time. "Basically, their whole world revolved around being there."

Kawaguchi saw the obsessive side of the Internet and managed to escape it.

Others aren't as lucky.

Jonathan Kandell, assistant director of the counseling center at the University of Maryland, has found that college students, especially those in the 18 to 22 age range – are quite susceptible to an Internet obsession.

Kandell, an assistant professor of psychology at Maryland, recently published his theories in the journal "CyberPsychology and Behavior."

The search for identity, the need for intimate relationships and the need for control often play a significant role in this potentially unhealthy behavior, Kandell said. Logging on, whether in chat rooms or through Web sites, can help students ranging academically from the inept to the astute cope with life's hardships.

"If it's fulfilling a need, it's hard to give it up," Kandell said.

And the free, high-speed access provided to students appears to make it easier for them than for other people to turn to the Internet as an escape.

Kandell was quick to note, however, that "addiction" was probably not the most accurate term in these cases. He compared overuse of the Internet to compulsive behaviors such as pathological gambling.

"I do see it as a psychological dependency," Kandell said.

Kandell's evidence is mostly anecdotal, culled from student clients and classrooms filled with students who say they're downloading to the point of distraction.

In one class he visited, between 70 and 80 percent of the students raised their hands when asked whether the Internet was their chief obstacle to concentrating on projects and papers.

Studies on other campuses have shown between 6 and 12 percent of students may be spending too much time online, thanks in part to the ease of campus Internet access.

"People are staying up all night, not going to class, not doing their homework – ultimately flunking out of school," Kandell said. 'It's more pervasive than people think."

Kandell said that for most people, like Kawaguchi, the novelty wears off. . . .

Kawaguchi sees both good and bad in the Internet. The native of Oahu, Hawaii, considers it an effective communication tool, but not a surrogate for human relationships.

"Personally, I wouldn't recommend someone going out to look for someone on the Internet," she said. "I completely lucked out.

Now she uses her Internet access to look things up and send electronic mail to friends and family. She hasn't gone to a chat room in over a year.

"It just gets boring after a while – the people on there are just complaining about the same things day in and day out," she said. "When it's new, it's really fun. After a while, you see this isn't reality."

Matt Gowen, *Lawrence Journal-World*.
Reprinted with permission.

3. Hourglass exercise

The hourglass should start with a hard-news lead. Then reconstruct the incident chronologically as in this original version.

Two bank couriers were hailed as heroes for helping authorities capture three suspects in a robbery at the Boatman's Bank of Pevely Tuesday.

One courier, Dennis Boushie, who lives near Festus, chased the suspect on foot. The other courier, Willie Moore of St. Louis, drove a bank van, chasing a getaway car.

Capt. Ed Kemp of the Jefferson County Sheriff's Department praised the couriers' actions: "This is beyond the call of duty. They act more like police officers than private citizens or bank couriers."

Boushie said he had asked the teller who was robbed if the robber had a weapon, and she had said he did not. He said his pursuit of the robber had been "just common sense."

Authorities gave this account:

A man entered the bank shortly after it opened Tuesday morning and shouted, "Give me the money or else!" A teller gave him an envelope containing money, and he ran out the front door.

Boushie chased him on foot, and, when the suspect jumped in a car, Boushie pointed the car out to Moore, who pursued it in a bank van. A few minutes later, Boushie got in a Pevely police patrol car and helped police track the getaway car.

Police broadcast a description of the the getaway car, which had continued north on I-55 carrying two men and a woman. Arnold police spotted the car, stopped it and arrested the three suspects.

Authorities say they found several thousand dollars in the car. The woman had stuffed money down her pants, they said.

Police were seeking federal warrants for the bank robbery.

Leo Fitzmaurice, *St. louis Post-Dispatch.* Reprinted with permission.

4. List technique exercise

The object of this exercise is to break the statistics into a bulleted list. Here is an example with the list format:

Americans use the Internet extensively without sacrificing their personal and social lives although users and non-users are concerned about privacy, a new study reveals.

The study, "Surveying the Digital Future," by Jeffrey Cole, director of the Center for Communication Policy at the University of California, examines how the Internet is affecting Americans' behavior and attitudes.

"Our findings refute many preconceived notions that persist about how the Internet affects our lives," Cole said. "Yet deeply rooted problems still exist that have long-range implications for this powerful technology."

Some findings from the study:
More than two-thirds of Americans have some type of access to the Internet.
- 54.6 percent use e-mail.
- 51.7 percent of Internet users make purchases online.
- 66 percent of users and 49.3 percent of non-users believe that

new technologies, including the Internet, have made the world a better place.

"Historically Americans have been quite concerned about their privacy," Cole said. "But those concerns focused on government intrusion in their lives. Today the concerns about privacy are quite different and focus directly on perceptions of private companies collecting information and tracking our movements on the Internet."

The study is part of the World Internet Project and is sponsored by the National Science Foundation.

5 and 6 Sections technique and Web story:

Self explanatory

Workbook Exercises

10-1. Endings

These exercises will give students practice using circle and future kickers. It's preferable to have students rewrite their own endings, but these will give students some idea of the concepts.

a. She often wonders where she would be if she had not read the magazine article about law school.

b. The last paragraph could be this future element:
He would like to eventually open a Batman museum. He would charge $1 admission only for one reason – so he could buy more Batman merchandise.

10-2. Bright endings

Students struggle with these exercises because it is difficult for them to write brights, but these really stress the need to devise good endings. Here are some examples from students' work:

a. Food stamps

> They say you can't take it with you when you die, but you just might be able to get food stamps. After Albert Maxwell died, he received this letter from the Department of Social Services: "Your food stamps will be stopped effective in January because we received a notice that you passed away."
>
> The letter went on to say, "You may reapply if there is a change in your circumstances. May God bless you."
> Linda Starrett, University of Kansas

b. Burglar

> He had too much to drink and he was hungry. So a 24-year-old Lawrence man decided to get a pizza Sunday night.
>
> But when he broke into the cooler at Domino's pizza parlor, 1700 W. 23 St., all he found were three containers of pizza sauce, 10 pounds of mozzarella cheese and two sacks of flour. Self service.
>
> He was arrested when the store manager, who lives across the street, called the police.
>
> Maybe next time he'll have his pizza delivered. - Linda Starrett, University of Kansas

c. Gorillas

> Like humans, like primates. Gorillas may be an endangered species, but that doesn't mean that a female gorilla will mate with just anyone, no way.
>
> That's what officials at the Pittsburgh Zoo have learned the past 14 months as they attempted to mate a 22-year-old female to visiting males to breed the zoo's first gorilla born in captivity.
>
> The female gorilla had ignored two suitors and punched her former roommate, an aggressive high-strung Silverback, before falling for a genteel Westerner from Colorado Springs.
>
> This time the zoo is optimistic. They say different females like different types. Does that surprise anyone?
> Scherry Sweeney, University of Kansas

10-3. Inverted pyramid

The lead should say that tear gas was set off at the middle school and that the incident forced the school to close. The lead or the second sentence should include injuries. The impact on people involved with the school should be placed high in the story. Here is the original, which you may distribute and have students compare with their own stories:

Tear gas routes Portland pupils

Vandals set off a canister of tear gas inside Gregory Heights Middle School Thursday morning, sending at least 48 children and two teachers to a dozen Portland hospitals for treatment.

The school was evacuated and closed for the day. Officials said they suspected the tear gas was released in a main corridor of the school, which has more than 900 staff members and students in the 6th, 7th and 8th grades. Three students were being sought for questioning.

The problem caused no evacuation of homes in the neighborhood around the school at Northeast 73rd Avenue and Siskiyou Street. Students and teachers vomited and suffered a number of other problems, including a burning sensation in the lungs, nose, throat and eyes, due to the gas that apparently was released in a school corridor.

Portland Fire Bureau spokesman Don Mayer said he didn't know of anyone who was in serious or critical condition. The trips to the hospital, he said, were precautionary.

More than a dozen ambulances were sent to the school to take children, ages 12 to 15, to local hospitals.

The fire department was called at 9:31 a.m., and a second alarm was sounded at 10:32.

Principal John Alkire said the substance was in the science and math hall area in the northwest corner of the school's first floor. He said the substance was odorless.

"It was like walking into an irritating wall," he said.

Students were taken to an area on the front lawn of the school. They were carried by stretcher or walked to ambulances.

Richard Harder, a paramedic with the Portland Fire Bureau, was one of the first to arrive. He saw about 15 children on the ground, some of them with severe respiratory problems. Others were coughing vomiting and sneezing.

Carol Palumbo, an eighth-grade teacher, was consoling crying students in front of the school after the evacuation. "The kids are really upset. It's just horrendous, whatever it was," she said.

Mayer said a Mace-like container was given to investigators by a parent who said it was sold to her son on the school ground Thursday morning. Mace is a type of tear gas.

Mayer also said the school officials gave them three names of possible suspects. Investigators were trying to reach those youths.

Autumn Gierlich, 13, an eighth-grader who suffers from asthma, was coughing and receiving oxygen shortly after the incident. As she waited for an ambulance, she said: "I got the stuff into my lungs, and I could barely breathe. I had to gasp for air. I was dizzy. Now I'm feeling better. They gave me oxygen. I coughed and coughed, and spit up phlegm."

Jessie Doty, 12, a seventh grader, said: "I started coughing. It just stung my throat. My eyes watered and turned red."

Jeff MacMillan, 12, a seventh-grader, said he got a headache from the chemical. But he said other classmates were worse off, including one girl who fainted and had to be carried from the building.

The Fire Bureau began allowing staff members to return inside about noon.

"The symptoms the kids are exhibiting are consistent with Mace," Mayer said.

Ambulances took children from the school to a dozen Portland hospitals, including Providence Medical Center, Emanuel Hospital & Health Center, Woodland Park Hospital, University Hospital, Bess Kaiser, Portland Adventist Medical Center and St. Vincent Hospital and Medical Center.

The students who were not affected by the fumes were sent home about 10:45 a.m., said Michael Grice, spokesman for the Portland Public Schools. The school district sent buses to take the students home.

Classes at the school will resume Friday morning, Grice said.

Thirteen-year-old Nguyen Do, an eighth grader, was in class during the morning break. He and others went out in the hall and started coughing.

"So I covered my mouth and ran out of the building," Do said. "It's Mace. I know that. It was a set-up to get out of the class or something."

Dave Hogan and Paul Koberstein, *The Oregonian.* Reprinted with permission.

10-4. *Wall Street Journal* formula

Here is an abbreviated version of the story. Note the anecdotal lead followed by a nut graph explaining that Karen Malloy is one of many frustrated by voice mail. The backup includes examples of companies that abandoned voice mail. The ending does not return to the person in the lead, but it returns to the concept in the lead.

Voice mail taps wrath of callers

After Karen Malloy, 48, of St. Louis fell down steps recently and wrenched her back, she phoned her doctor. All she got was voice mail – a computerized recording that said the doctor wasn't available.

Because she couldn't get the doctor's OK for an emergency-room visit, her insurer refused to pay the $350 charge. Malloy retaliated by changing doctors.

[Nut graph]

Her frustration with voice mail, shared by millions daily, reflects a growing disenchantment with the technology.

About 85 percent of Fortune 500 firms and 2 million smaller companies are using voice mail, and the $1 billion-a-year voice mail business is still growing 20 percent a year.

But customers increasingly complain about being stuck on the phone listening to a computerized voice or leaving messages that are never returned. A recent survey by Plog research found that 56 percent of consumers have at some point given up trying to reach a company because of frustrations with voice mail. Those concerns are forcing some companies to rethink or abandon voice-mail technology:

- Hickory Printing Group in Hickory, N.C., has axed voice mail because "customers hated it," says CEO Thomas Reese. His revenue is running 10 percent ahead of the $27 million level a year ago, and he credits the human touch.
- Delta Air Lines experimented with voice mail, and some departments – including public relations – discarded it.

Says Delta spokesman Bill Berry: "We quickly decided we wanted nothing to do to with it. If you call, I don't want you to speak to a mechanical voice."

NBC-TV tried using voice mail featuring a lengthy electronic menu at its studios in Burbank, Calif. "It was awful," says Rick Romo, West Coast producer of "Today." It infuriated publicists, advertisers and anyone else who called. Two weeks ago NBC dumped it and returned to live operators.

Managers who bought the technology thought they'd save money. "What they saw was the bottom line. They didn't realize it would drive people nuts," Romo says.

Many companies use voice mail as an electronic gatekeeper, routing calls through a main number and an automated attendant. You hear a recording and choose from a menu of departments or services. But it can take a minute or more to go through all the options. This can result in a hefty tab if you happen to be calling long distance.

Complaining about voice mail isn't easy either. Who do you call? The Federal Communications Commission? The Better Business Bureau? Both use voice mail.

Melinda Ayala, 40, of Hollywood, Fla., tried to call the Better Business Bureau every day for a week.

"I just couldn't get through," says Ayala. "They say, 'Press 2.' You get a busy signal. A recording says, 'Press 5' to be put on hold. You could go on and on with this all day. I don't think it's any way to run a business."

Despite its drawbacks, voice mail seems here to stay. As companies downsize to cope with tough economic times, many use voice mail to trim payroll costs or shift operators into other roles.

A company can buy a voice-mail system for $10,000 to $800,000 and can often recoup that investment within 24 hours. Or it can pay the phone company a flat monthly fee for a voice-mail service.

Beyond saving money, voice mail makes message-taking more accurate because it eliminates human error. . . .

"Once you get used to voice mail, it's irreplaceable," says spokesman Bob Powers of the Institute for Electrical and Electronics Engineers.

But others argue that nothing can soothe a customer like the human voice.

Phyllis Rosen, 48, a receptionist and phone operator at Lyons Financial Group in Charlotte, N.C., says, "I can make or break sales that come into this company by speaking directly to the people that call, by trying to console them. I don't think a machine can do that. It's a very cold way of dealing with people."

10-5. Hourglass exercise

Compare your story with this original version. This story starts with a hard news lead and the basic facts. The hourglass chronology begins in the middle when the writer recounts the incident in a narrative form.

Student's version:

Darren Nitz said he didn't think much about the fire above his apartment Monday morning until he heard that two neighbor boys were trapped in their apartment.

Nitz said he put one of the boys, 14-year-old Michael Fuson, on his back and carried him outside. Nitz and another neighbor, Brad Lindsey, were unable to reach the boy's brother who was trapped in his bedroom. Ten-year-old Kenneth Fuson died in the fire.

Michael Fuson is in critical condition at Emanuel Hospital and Health Center's burn unit with second- and third-degree burns over a third of his body.

Boy dies in fire; brother rescued

A 10-year-old boy died and his older brother was burned over a third of his body Monday when a searing fire swept through their Southeast Portland apartment, where they'd apparently been left alone.

A neighbor was able to pull Michael Fuson, 14, from the apartment at 15758 S.E. Division St. but was unable to reach 10-year-old Kenneth A. J. Fuson in his bedroom.

Michael Fuson was in critical condition at Emanuel Hospital and Health Center's burn unit with second- and third-degree burns on his hands, arms, face, neck, back, buttocks and thighs. He was breathing with the help of a ventilator.

The children's mother, Linda Lee Fuson, arrived at the 32-unit apartment complex after the firefighters, who were on the scene at 6:39 a.m., said Neil Heesacker, a spokesman for the Portland Fire Bureau. Officials did not know Monday morning where she had been.

Firefighters sifted through the rubble looking for a cause of the blaze that was hot enough to burn through the floor, blister the gypsum board walls and melt the family's television set. Three pet birds also died.

A fire investigator credited a neighbor, Darren Nitz, 31, with saving Michael Fuson's life. Nitz lives on the first floor of the Anderson Villa apartments; the Fuson's home was one floor above.

Hourglass format starts here

About 6:35 a.m. Nitz heard neighbors pounding on his door and yelling about the fire. He didn't think much about it at first, Nitz said, until someone said two children were trapped in the apartment. Michael was about seven feet from his bedroom door, lying as though he'd been crawling toward the front door.

"He was saying, 'I can't, I can't' and rolling over and over," Nitz said. "I said, 'We've got to get out of here.' "

Nitz tried to grab hold of the youth's arm but couldn't because he was so badly burned. So Nitz put the youth over his shoulder and carried him outside. Michael told his rescuer that Kenneth still was upstairs.

Nitz went back to the top of the stairs, but the flames had reached the front door. Another neighbor, Brad Lindsey, 24, grabbed a fire extinguisher at the bottom of the stairs and followed on Nitz' heels.

"It was fully going when we got up there," Lindsey said. "Just after we got up there, it just vacuumed and shot right across" the stairway.

Lindsey and Nitz retreated back down the stairs.

"There was no way either of us could do anything about it," Lindsey said.

Firefighters brought the fire under control at 7:04 a.m., 15 minutes after a second-alarm sent additional firefighters and equipment.

The blaze caused an estimated $50,000 damage to the building and $10,000 damage to the apartment contents. Fire officials estimated the value of the building at $480,000 and the family's belongings at $80,000.

The fire also caused smoke damage to the apartment of Pat and Lisa Hampton, who live across the stairs from Linda Fuson. Lisa Hampton is Fuson's sister.

Heesacker said fire in an enclosed area such as an apartment can push temperatures to 1,700 degrees Fahrenheit near the ceiling and 1,000 degrees on the floor.

Holley Gilbert, *The Oregonian*. Reprinted with permission.

10-6. List technique

Here is the original story:

Post-secondary education pays big dividends

Get a degree after high school and your income goes up by degrees, too – averaging $1,000 a month more for people with sheepskins than a high school diploma, a new study says.

In *What's It Worth*, the Census Bureau also says more adults than ever – 25.2 percent – now have a post-high school degree of some type, anything from a trade school certificate to a professional degree. That's up from 20.7 percent in 1984, says study author Rebecca Sutterlin.

The report, based on surveys of 23,000 households last year, confirmed education's impact on earnings potential, but also showed racial disparities. Among the findings:

Those with post-high school degrees earned an average of $2,231 monthly, compared with $1,280 for those with some college but no degree, $1,077 for those with a high school diploma and just $492 for those who don't have a high school education.

On average, blacks earn significantly less than whites at each educational level, with the exception of those with master's degrees. Blacks with bachelor's degrees, for instance, earned an average of $1,814 a month, compared with $2,149 for whites.

• 26.4 percent of whites have college degrees, compared with 14 percent of blacks and 11.6 percent of Hispanics

• 19.4 percent of white adults over 18 hadn't finished high school, compared with 31.9 percent of blacks and 43.8 percent of Hispanics.

• 5 percent of men had degrees in engineering, only 2 percent of women did.

Dennis Kelly, *USA Today*. Copyright 1993. Reprinted with permission.

10-7. Style test

Correct the errors in the following sentences.

1. The government estimates more than 11,000 sea turtles drown in shrimp nets in waters in the U.S. **United States)** each year.

2. A shrimper was imprisoned for failing to use a federally mandated **(no hyphen with ly words)** turtle protection device on his boat.

3. The store was at 1,202 **(1202 no comma)** Maple Rd. **(Road)**.

4. There were 10 lbs. **(pounds)** of cheese and four lbs. **(4 pounds)** of tomatoes in the refrigerator.

5. Houston Police Sergeant Roy House said the suspect defrauded employers out of $150,000 ~~dollars.~~ **(no dollars)**.

6. The United States Department of Agriculture **(U.S. Department of Agriculture)** employs 7,000 meat inspectors.

7. The USDA **(correct on second reference - no periods)** operates a training center at College Station, Texas, **(add comma and don't abbreviate)** where veterinarians attended classes.

8. The defendent **(defendant)** was convicted of possessing three **(3)** ounces of cocaine.

9. The story was about a woman with Alzheimers Disease. **(Alzheimer's disease)**.

10. The female gorilla is from the east coast **(East Coast)**.

Storytelling and Feature Techniques

11

Goals

- To teach students descriptive and narrative writing techniques
- To teach students how to apply storytelling to news and feature stories

This chapter is designed to teach students how to make all kinds of stories more interesting by using storytelling techniques. Students need to understand that before they can use descriptive and narrative writing techniques, they must think about them during the reporting process. Reinforce the concepts of curiosity and observation for show-in-action writing and the need to gather more details than students think they will need so they can reconstruct an event for narrative writing. Check the Web site for this book for many links to good storytelling resources: *http://info.wadsworth.com/rich.*

Teaching Suggestions

This chapter is fun to teach because students usually enjoy the chance to express some creativity in their writing. After you explain some of the descriptive and narrative techniques, ask students to start reading their newspapers analytically by looking for these techniques. Students can overdo the descriptive writing, however. It is important to stress that some stories, particularly breaking news about serious events, may lend themselves more to a hard-news approach. You also need to caution students to use description sparingly and only when it is appropriate to the subject matter.

Discussion for most of the textbook activities can be based on your students' examples. You could read the best ones or ask them to read some of their paragraphs.

Textbook Exercises

1. Scene

This is a good exercise to do during class, especially on nice day. Ask students to go to any place in your school or on campus and take notes observing people in action; then have them return to class and write description of the scene, including any dialogue they may have overheard. I once assigned this on Valentine's Day, and the students got some wonderful snatches of dialogue and vignettes. If you lack enough time in class, you could assign it for homework.

2. Analogies

Write a list of nouns on the board and ask students to write similes and metaphors, or ask them to observe a scene and write their own analogies. For example, one student observed a trash can with a red Coke can on the edge and described it as a toy soldier guarding the contents of the trash can. Students enjoy going out (especially during class) to find their own analogies. To save time, however, you could give them a list such as: snow, cotton, spaghetti. Another variation is to bring in some items such as cotton, spaghetti, a rock, and so on. Ask students to close their eyes and feel the objects. Then ask them to describe the objects with analogies.

3. Narrative writing

This is one of the best activities I have used. The writing the students do is poignant. Suggest that students interview each other about a traumatic or emotional incident in their lives. Students are surprisingly candid about their experiences, and they seem to enjoy the interviewing process for this exercise. Some examples are car accidents, arrests for drunken driving, first day of college, and birth of a baby.

To teach this form of writing, stress that students must seek details such as the type of car a person was driving, what the person was wearing, what the person was thinking at the time of the event. I often demonstrate how to do this by asking one student to reconstruct verbally the events of his or her morning for the class. Then I ask specific questions, such as: What time did you get out of bed? Did you awaken to an alarm? What did you have for breakfast? What type of cereal? And so on.

4. Web storytelling

Personal storytelling abounds on the Web. Although inverted pyramid is recommended for news stories, the Web offers a chance for students to be creative and to try many different story forms. Students can adapt the previous exercise to the Web by writing the story in a chunk-style essay or narrative with cliffhanger endings at the bottom of each chunk.

5. Timed free writing

Lucille deView, former writing coach for *The Orange County Register,* said she discovered timed writing exercises in a fiction class and used the technique to become more creative in storytelling and coaching. In an article in the former *Coaches Corner* (September 1994), deView said she had wonderful experience using this with a group at one of her writing seminars. In one case she just asked, "What is your favorite Campbell's soup?" Chicken noodle won, and the writers produced some wonderful stories about their childhood memories of chicken soup. The main point of this exercise is to get students writing and creating. Don't grade these exercises for grammar or anything else. This type of writing exercise is a good way to let students exercise their creativity.

Workbook Exercises

11-1. Storytelling mindset exercises

These exercises are also good for getting students to take risks and explore storytelling. You need to stress that they can't take liberties with facts in real newswriting. Many writing coaches and teachers use fiction very successfully as a way of teaching news storytelling. These exercises also are fun for students. They work best as class activities that should not be graded.

11-2. Storytelling for a crime story

This exercise will give students a chance to use narrative storytelling techniques for what could be a routine police story. The exercise is fairly simple and could be used with beginning students as well as advanced students.

Here is the original story. For pure narrative writing, you could start with the third paragraph:

Mall shopper robbed by man hiding in car

Holiday shopping and holiday robbing often go hand in hand.

Pauline Cayia of Fort Lauderdale can testify to that.

Cayia finished shopping at the Galleria mall about 7 p.m. on Sunday, she said.

When she got into her unlocked car, she said, she smelled a strong body odor. As she drove away from the shopping center at 2700 E. Sunrise Blvd., a man popped up in the back seat and demanded her purse.

"I was in the mall about an hour and a half," Cayia said. "Before I got in the car, I looked around and didn't see anything. I smelled an odor when I put my packages in the front seat, and I checked the back seat, but I didn't see anybody.

"I suppose he was sleeping, because he didn't say anything until I got to Federal Highway."

Cayia, who manages a recording studio, said the robber was polite and well-spoken.

"He said, 'Ma'am, give me your purse and let me off here.' I started going fast to try and attract the attention of a policeman but didn't find anybody to stop me," Cayia said. "I was going fast, and he said, 'You're going to kill us.'"

As Cayia headed south along Federal Highway toward Broward Boulevard, the robber went through her purse.

"He said, 'Here's your purse' and threw it into the front seat, but he kept my wallet," Cayia said.

At Federal and Broward, Cayia slowed to turn and ended up hitting a car. At that point, the robber jumped out and ran, even though the car was still moving. Cayia drove directly to the police station.

"I don't know if I was scared or in control. I just wanted to get the police, Cayia said.

On Monday, she got a call that her wallet had been found. It was returned along with her credit cards and driver's license. Only her $85 in cash was missing.

The suspect is described as a white man about 27 years old, 5 feet 7 inches tall with brown hair and brown eyes, clean-shaven but unkempt.

Ardy Frieberg, *Sun-Sentinel* (Fort Lauderdale, Fla.). Reprinted with permission.

11-3. Storytelling news feature

This exercise should emphasize the value of gathering good details. Here is Alan Richman's version. This is a column, so Richman can use the first-person voice and add some personal comments that you could not use in a news story. Discuss what difference details make in the story.

The $10,000 lesson

Michael Yanelli did not steal the $10,000.

He found the $10,000.

He stole a car with $10,000 in the glove compartment. He admits that. He has been caught stealing cars four times now, so the confession does not come hard.

"It's a habit with me," he says.

He did not have to hot-wire any of the cars, although, as a graduate of Boston Technical High School and a resident of East Boston, he has spent plenty of time in environments where such a skill can be learned.

"All the cars had keys in them," Yanelli says. "Tell people to leave their cars locked up and don't leave $10,000 in the car where anybody can get it."

Currently, Yanelli is not living in East Boston. He is residing in the Charles Street Jail. On the evening of Saturday, July 2, he was arrested and charged with stealing a 1979 Cadillac from outside the Brandywyne Village apartments in East Boston. Yanelli took the car Thursday, two days before his arrest.

"There was a briefcase in the front seat with $60 in it. The tank was empty, so I went for gas. I put $20 in and got half a tank."

Nobody ever said operating a stolen Cadillac was cheap.

"I opened the glove compartment, looking for something to blow my nose. I threw out a white envelope. Twenties and 50s and 100s piled out. My heart went 90 miles an hour."

The white envelope contained $10,000 in cash.

Yanelli bought two first-class airline tickets to Las Vegas for himself and a friend, a color television set as a wedding present for his best friend, a $1,700 Sony television for the mother and father of a friend, a Sears television for his mother, $600 in clothes, a watch, a ring, a radio, basketball shoes and four Beatles tapes.

Everybody accepted with thanks except his mother, who refused to take the television, and the friend who was supposed to go to Las Vegas but couldn't take off from work.

"I spent the money on true friends," he says.

On Thursday he went to the dog track at Wonderland, where he lost a few hundred dollars. On Friday, he went to the horse track at Suffolk Downs, where he won $1,500, hitting the 10th race perfecta of Fleet Concessioner and Marshua's Romeo. He and a friend celebrated at the Kowloon restaurant in Saugus, where they had four pu-pu platters.

Only then did he ditch the car.

The people I talked to in East Boston – a young lady with lavender eye shadow, three women at the Brandywyne apartment complex, a few cops at the District 7 station, workers at the East Boston District Court – all had the same things to say about Yanelli's ride: If he had just gotten rid of the car and kept the money, he probably would never have been caught.

Yeah, I know, I know," he says, raising his voice in exasperation. "My brother said, 'Get rid of the car.' I even drove to Revere on Thursday, to Cerretani's parking lot, wiped my fingerprints off the car. I was throwing the keys away. I hesitated. I needed a couple more things."

He thinks the owner of the Cadillac, Rene Gignac of Laconia, N.H., saw him driving the car and picked out his picture from a book of mug shots. People from his neighborhood, maybe those few who didn't get color televisions, tipped off police that a 22-year-old unemployed man living above Carlo's Cold Cut Centre on Bennington Street was spending more money than people who live above cold cut stores ordinarily spend.

"Tommy and Johnny, two cops who arrested me before, came to my house," he says. "They told me I might as well admit it. They're good cops. I gave them the rest of the money. I told them where the car was."

He isn't so sure he should be punished for spending the money Gignac left in an unlocked glove compartment of an unlocked Cadillac with the keys in the ignition.

"This guy is completely stupid," Yanelli says. "I'm down on this guy. It's his fault."

Apparently Gignac needed the money to close a real estate deal. That doesn't explain why he needed it in cash. I tried to telephone him, but he has an unlisted number.

A man can't be too careful these days.

Alan Richman, *The Boston Globe*. Reprinted with permission.

Public Relations Writing 12

Goals

- To learn how to write news releases for print and broadcast
- To learn how to write news releases for the Web
- To learn how to plan a media kit

Teaching Suggestions

This chapter is intended to give students a broad idea of public relations writing. Stress that students should study the audience for their material. If they are writing for newspaper or broadcast editors, they should get to the point quickly. If you want to give students an idea of the types of press releases the local newspaper receives, you can ask an editor to save some for a week and have students compare the releases to the information the newspaper used. Many of the releases sent to a newspaper are very poorly written, and you could use them for rewrite activities. Encourage students to think visually by planning photographs, charts and illustrations to accompany their materials. If they are writing the release to be posted on the Web, they should also strive for brevity, limiting the release to one or two screens (about 15 to 20 lines of type per screen, depending on the font and type size).

The Web site for this book offers some good resources about techniques of writing public relations materials: *http://info.wadsworth.com/rich.*

Textbook Exercises

1. Campus event press release

Ask students to check bulletin boards at your school for information about events and write press releases for them, or ask students to call various organizations on campus or in the community for the information. Many organizations would be grateful to have help, and you might assign students to volunteer as publicists for some local groups, as though they had a beat.

2. Devise a media kit

This can be a major project for students. You can make this assignment extensive by asking students to include a backgrounder, a fact sheet, a news release and graphic devices, or just asking them to plan the kit. If students are going to interview clients, make sure each student has a different client unless you are planning to do this as a class project. Or you could invite a company official to class and have students do the same research. (A related but more thorough exercise is listed in workbook exercises for this chapter.)

3. Write a news release

This exercise is fun for students and encourages them to be creative. Limit the release to one page but ask students to think of an enticing headline. If they use a creative lead, remind them to get the main idea in the second sentence or paragraph.

4. E-mail news release

This news release should feature a bulleted list for the numbers, which is recommended for Web writing. For e-mail releases, tell students to put the contact information at the top and bottom of the release, including phone contacts as well as e-mail. The length of the release should be limited to two screens, which may be limited to fewer than 150 words, depending on the font and size.

5. Public service announcement

This exercise gives students practice writing very brief public service announcements. This one from the Federal Emergency Management Agency is about 15 to 20 seconds:

When a thunderstorm moves through your area, be alert for tornadoes. Tornadoes have three danger signs: Before a tornado hits, the wind may die down and the air may become very still. Two - tornadoes can be nearly invisible, marked only by swirling debris at the base of the funnel. Three - tornadoes generally occur near the trailing edge of a thunderstorm. This is a public service message from the Federal Emergency Management Agency.

6. Promote a product

Students can be very creative with this exercise. Let students make up a product or give them one, such as mustard, to promote. One group of students in my class created a cola product with Viagra and wrote a fun release.

Workbook Exercises

12-1. Qualities of news releases

Answers can vary. The important point is to make students think critically about news qualities releases should have such as timeliness, proximity, human interest, conflict or any other qualities of news. For broadcast, students should include visuals as a primary requirement. News releases must contain the contact information (company name and address, contact name, phone and e-mail), For Immediate Release (or a release date). Students should also practice writing headlines.

Web press releases MUST contain e-mail addresses. A big problem with Web releases is that they often do not include company phone numbers and addresses. Stress to students that an anonymous Webmaster is not good p.r. People also like to be able to contact companies by phone or mail. Web releases should contain posting dates as well.

Student enjoy clicking into Web sites, so the latter part of this exercise will give them a chance to compare Web releases and discuss the differences. I would rather encourage discussion but if you prefer, you can ask them to write their analysis.

12-2. Gather information and write news releases

This exercise will give students a chance to gather their own information. Even if some of the information on bulletin boards is in news release form, it probably is not in good form. The print and fax form should follow standard instructions as in the textbook. The broadcast form should include visual opportunities. The Web and e-mail forms should have the contact information at the top but related links and posting dates at the bottom. These last two should be as brief as possible. The contact information should also be listed at the bottom of the e-mail release.

12-3. Rewrite a news release

This is a very poorly written press release, the type many local newspapers receive. It should be reduced to one simple paragraph with the basic information. Eliminate the "To whom it may concern" salutation. Students may list the organization name and contact information on the left side of the release or design a heading for stationery. Here is an example:

Big Brothers/Big Sisters of Douglas County, Inc.
220 Main St., Lawrence, Kansas 04040   (913) 454-1222

FOR IMMEDIATE RELEASE

March 13, Year
Contact: George Hand
454-1222

BIG BROTHERS/BIG SISTERS SEEKS VOLUNTEERS

Big Brothers/Big Sisters of Douglas County, Inc. is seeking volunteers to provide adult companionship to children. The organization will conduct an informational meeting for prospective volunteers at 10 a.m. Saturday, March 13 at the organization's office, 220 Main St. in Lawrence. For people unable to attend the first meeting, another informational meeting will be at 6 p.m. Sunday, March 14 at the same location.

12-4. News release

The statistics in this exercise can be written in list form or students can suggest a graphic. This release lends itself to a chart, preferably a graphic that could be reprinted in a newspaper. In lieu of a graphic, you could itemize the statistics in column form as indicated here. The letterhead from the university public relations office includes the word "news release," but it can be within the body of the letter. Note the name of the writer, who differs from the director, at the end of the release.

News Release   **Name of University**

Office of University Relations, University Relations Center, City, State, ZIP code
(913) 000-0000 * Fax (913) 000-0000

Date   Tom Hutton, Director of News
For Immediate Release

MINORITY ENROLLMENT UP AT --- UNIVERSITY

CITY IN CAPITAL LETTERS – Minority enrollment increased 8.7 percent this fall at the University of ___. The increase came in a year when overall campus enrollment grew less than 1 percent.

"This university has taken a significant step forward," said Chancellor Gene A. Budig. "Our many efforts of recent years are beginning to produce the desired results."

Enrollment of black students increased by 34 students to 678. American Indian student enrollment showed the largest increase – 46 – to a total of 204. Asian student enrollment increased by 44, to 565. Hispanic student enrollment grew by 29, to 452.

"The increase in minority students is a gratifying sight for the many students, faculty and administrators who have worked for it," Budig said. "We still have more to do. This is only the beginning."

The enrollment categories are based on self-reported student data.

Minority Enrollment at the University of ------

5 years ago	Last year	This year
1,540	1,747	1,899

Story by Robin Eversole, (913) 000-0000

12-5. News feature release

This release is rather long, and the exercise is poorly organized. Using all the information in double-spacing would exceed two pages. Tell students to make some decisions about what they think can be deleted. Here is the original release (printed here in single space but should be double-spaced for release) and a newspaper story based on it. Compare it with the newspaper story and note what information the writer used from the release and what the writer gathered independently. This release was sent with a package of other releases and a News Tips sheet of teasers – a technique that is helpful to editors. Here is the teaser, followed by the full release:

ADDICTION TO TESTS

A bad grade may be the least of your worries when taking tests, says a KU anthropology professor whose recent book, "Testing, Testing: Social Consequences of the Examined Life," challenges America's addiction to drug, intelligence, aptitude and integrity tests.

News Release
The University of Kansas

Office of University Relations, University Relations Center, Lawrence, KS 66045
(913) 000-0000 * Fax (913) 000-0000

Month, Day, Year
For Immediate Release

Tom Hutton, Director of News

TESTS MAY NOT BE GOOD FOR YOU

LAWRENCE – American society is addicted to tests, according to F. Allan Hanson, professor of anthropology at the University of Kansas.

In his new book, "Testing Testing: Social Consequences of the Examined Life," Hanson uncovers a variety of hidden consequences of tests commonly used in business and education. He recommends eliminating most drug tests, intelligence and aptitude tests, and lie detector or integrity tests.

"The American preoccupation with testing has resulted in a panoply of techniques dedicated to scanning, probing, weighing, perusing and recording every last detail of our personal traits and life experiences," Hanson says.

The future is likely to produce even more detailed knowledge of each individual as new genetic tests and DNA fingerprinting are developed, he says.

Because tests provide information about people, they serve as devices of power for agencies – employers, educational administrators, insurance firms, law enforcement agencies – to determine whom to employ, to admit to college, to take on as a risk or to arrest.

"People are examined and evaluated less for qualifications or knowledge they already possess than for what the test results can predict about future actions or potential behavior," Hanson says.

Tests that measure performance, such as what a student has learned in class or skills mastered for a job are useful, he says. But tests that predict behavior or aptitude, such as IQ tests, have unintended and undesirable consequences, he says. Scores from IQ tests can become life sentences for children with very high or very low scores. Tests assign people to various categories – genius, slow learner, security risk – "where they are then treated, act and come to think of themselves according to the expectations associated with those categories," Hanson says.

"Decisions are made about people not on the basis of what they have done, or even what they certainly will do, but in terms of what they might do."

Employers use drug testing and integrity testing to screen applicants and monitor employees.

Hanson recommends eliminating integrity testing and using drug tests only when people are suspected of using drugs.

An exception is testing for anabolic steroids. Because the effects of steroids remain long after the drug can be detected by tests, Hanson says, "random testing is about the only way we can discover the use of the drug in athletic competition."

Of all forms of testing, Hanson finds lie detector tests the vilest, a pornographic gaze into a person's private thoughts. The test taker is powerless to conceal or control anything, and the test results are often unreliable, he says. Yet people whose character may be under public scrutiny submit to and even request polygraph tests to establish credibility.

Hanson says it should be possible to eliminate much of the testing used to predict behavior and aptitudes. For example, some college admission offices no longer require scores from aptitude tests, such as the American College Test (ACT) or Scholastic Aptitude Tests (SAT). Harvard Business School has dropped the Graduate Management Aptitude Tests (GMAT) as an application requirement.

In the Feb. 28, 1993 New York Times Book Review, Richard Flaste writes of Hanson's book: "What he brings to the arguments is surprising vivacious writing. He is splendid in pointing out the absurdities hidden in the various testing systems. The author brings to his often impassioned discussion of testing a fine humanism that accepts the need of societies' institutions to know something about people but that deplores the warping of the tools of assessment into prying, fearsome, demeaning instruments."

"Testing Testing" is published by the University of California Press and is available at local bookstores or by contacting Denise Cicourel at UC Press, 2120 Berkeley Way, Berkeley, CA 94720.

Story by Mary Jane Dunlap [phone number].

Office of University Relations, University of Kansas. Reprinted with permission.

Compare the news release with this newspaper story:

KU Professor's book puts tests to the test

Taking tests is an inevitable part of life, right?

One KU professor thinks we are overtested and wrote a book to prove his point.

F. Allan Hanson, professor of anthropology and author of "Testing Testing: Social Consequences of the Examined Life," says he thinks tests have established how our society's beliefs are established.

He cites 16th and 17th century tests for witchcraft to illustrate his point.

Back then, the ankles and feet of a suspected witch were tied together. The suspected witch was then thrown in to a lake. If she survived, she was a witch. If she drowned, she wasn't.

"The fact of doing that test established for society that witches exist," Hanson says.

He says the same thing is happening today with the idea of intelligence.

"I argue that the very concept of intelligence is the product of intelligence tests," he says.

Tests such as the SAT, ACT or IQ establish intelligence as a fixed number that people are stuck with for life, when intelligence really is the sum of many factors that can change, Hanson says.

"You begin to get a sense of yourself from those tests and act in a way that reflects them," he says. "It's kind of a life sentence for a 6-year-old to be called mediocre or genius."

Hanson, who has been teaching at KU since 1966, does not have a problem with tests that measure learned knowledge. He does have a problem with tests that establish ideas about future performance.

In "Testing Testing," which was reviewed in Sunday's New York Times, Hanson addresses drug testing.

Hanson says it is ironic that heroin, cocaine and barbiturates clear out of the system in a few days, while marijuana, a less destructive drug, stays for much longer.

He says pre-employment tests are problematic because the subjects know the test is coming and have the chance to stop using the more destructive drugs.

Hanson says that with any kind of observation a supervisor would be able to detect drug use anyway.

Ezra Wolfe, *The University Daily Kansan*. Reprinted with permission.

12-6. Web news release

The release from this site was poorly written with the name of the company repeated many times. However, the site is real and students should be encouraged to click to it from links on the book's Web site or directly so they can gain new ideas. An online news release might look like this:

Company: AccessNewAge.com http://www.accessnewage.com
Date: Today's date
Contact: YOUR NAME, PHONE AND E-MAIL ADDRESS

FOR IMMEDIATE RELEASE

Free Online Astrological Greeting Cards

Access:NewAge, an online company for spiritual and New Age products, is expanding its services by offering free, online personalized astrological greeting cards.

You can now send friends, lovers, and family an astrological message tailored just to them. Some examples: Happy Birthday Sagittarian . . .or Libra . . . or Gemini. Congratulations Pisces. I love you Taurus. Good luck Leo.

Each card contains an astrological profile and a link to an up-to-date monthly horoscope. Senders may select their greetings and choose special backgrounds.

Bob Siegel, webmaster at www.accessnewage.com, says "Access: NewAge was created with the intent of offering content on all things esoteric, spiritual and metaphysical. Free customizable astrological greeting cards are the step. And, if visitors want to order a gift to go with the card, like a book or aromatherapy products, they can do that at our site."

The online company was launched in 1995 and currently boasts more than 30,000 visitors a day. If offers links to other esoteric, spiritual and New Age sites. The site's "Looking Deeper Magazine" offers visitors hundreds of online articles from top new age specialists and forecast from our resident astrologer.

Contact the company at (address, phone number, e-mail and Web site address).

12-7. Product promotion - print and Web

    This is a very short release written in basic hard-news style. The original release was four double-spaced paragraphs. Binney & Smith prints a facts sheet about the company on the cover of its media kits, but you may have added a paragraph about the company, such as the information about producing 2 million crayons and other products the company produces. The lead and second sentence are somewhat redundant. Ask students to critique the original.

    For the Web, add e-mail, company URL, links to the company at the bottom and a Web posting date. The release was double-spaced.

NEWS

FROM CRAYOLA® PRODUCTS

Binney & Smith Inc. 1100 Church Lane, P.O. Box 431

Easton, Pennsylvania 18044-0431   (215) 000-0000

For Immediate Release

Contact: Mark J. O'Brien

Media Communications Representative

(215) 000-0000 ext. 289

CRAYOLA INTRODUCES FIRST HIGHLIGHTERS FOR KIDS

EASTON, Pa. – Binney & Smith, maker of Crayola crayons and markers, is introducing the first set of highlighters designed specifically for kids.

    Crayola Screamin' Neons washable school highlighters were developed especially for children.   Research conducted by Binney & Smith revealed that children start using highlighters around the age of 8 and continue throughout their school years. It also indicated that children use highlighters for a wide variety of activities including: school papers, study sheets, plays, maps and reports. Tailoring a highlighter to the needs of children resulted in the development of Screamin' Neons.

    Bright, neon graphics on each highlighter "scream" kids and fun. Screamin' Neons feature a special rounded nib that allows a smooth flow of ink without noise or squeaking. A patented washable formula allows the ink to be washed from hands, face and most children's clothing.

    Screamin' Neons are non-toxic and available in a pack of four colors: glowing green, neon yellow, hot magenta and electric blue. Suggested retail is approximately $1.99.

12-8. Interviews for news release format

This is best done as a group project. Divide the class into groups and assign them to broadcast or print stations in your area. If you don't have enough, you could ask students to link to online outlets in the state and conduct the interviews by e-mail. Some broadcast stations prefer fax and/or print releases, while most newspapers still prefer print. But e-mail releases are gaining popularity, and this form of submission may grow. Students need to be learning how to think in multimedia formats.

12-9. Design a media kit

You can contact a nonprofit organization in your area such as the Society for the Prevention of Animals and get information about them. Then use the information to develop a media kit.

Another alternative is to design a media kit to promote your own department. To save time, you might do this as a group project and assign one group to compile the history or the department or organization, another to do the news releases, another to develop story ideas for the media and so on.

A third option is to have students research a company online. So many companies have thorough information on the Web. Students can compile a media kit in print format or even on the Web. For Web-savvy students, you might ask them to develop a Web media kit. All students should brainstorm how the print and Web products might differ. A goal is to teach students to think in terms of how they will deliver information in many formats in the future.

If you are teaching an introductory media course that includes advertising, have the students design an advertisement for the project as well.

12-10. Creative preview publicity planning

Barbara Brown, a successful public relations practitioner in Anchorage, Alaska, has created many innovative approaches to media coverage. When the Anchorage Public Library got a new voice mail system that she was instructed to promote, she devised a contest: Name the voice (of the recorded voice). It was incredibly successful. Her news release for another ordinary event – checking the depth of the ice for safety of ice skaters – invited the media to take the test. They did.

The Ice Isn't Thick Enough, Wanna Check?

Anchorage Parks & Beautification will be taking core samples of the ice on area lakes to determine its safety. We ask the media to join us:

WHEN: DATE AND TIME
WHERE: Westchester Lagoon
WHO: Ray Roberts, South Maintenance Supervisor
WHAT: The taking of core sample of the ice

The Anchorage Fire Department and the Department of Cultural & Recreational Services issue the following warning:

All lakes in the Anchorage area are **EXTREMELY DANGEROUS** and are **OFFICIALLY CLOSED** to all outdoor recreational activities, including hockey, ice fishing and ice skating. Closure of area lakes will remain in effect until the ice is at least 12 inches thick. When the ice has achieved this thickness, the following lakes will be maintained as skating rinks:

- Westchester Lagoon
- Goose Lake
- Jewel Lake
- Spenard Lake
- Cheney Lake

Other lakes may have underground springs, which result in soft, unpredictable ice. Stay on maintained lakes once proper ice thickness has been established.

###

Broadcast Writing

13

Goals

- To teach students how to write basic broadcast stories
- To teach students the importance of focus
- To teach students broadcast style

This chapter is intended to serve as an introduction to broadcast writing, but it cannot substitute for a complete course that broadcast journalists would need. However, the exercises will serve to acquaint students with some of the basics of the broadcast craft. John Broholm, broadcast professor at the University of Kansas, wrote several of these exercises and models for the workbook and manual. This edition of the workbook includes new exercises to sharpen students' skills in word choice and leads. Transcripts for television news shows are available at CNN and other sites linked to the Web site for this book and an interactive, self-graded test is also on the site: *http://info.wadsworth.com/rich.*

Teaching Suggestions

Writing from print exercises is not as effective for this chapter as working from oral and visual materials. If you have an opportunity to get unedited videotapes from local broadcast journalists, that would be a preferable way to have students write their own stories and packages. You could also ask students to view tapes of packages in a local newscast and write the teasers for them or turn them into on-camera readers for the anchors without sound bites. If you have audio and video capabilities in your computer lab, you can link to CNN, MSNBC or many other radio and television online sites and hear audio clips.

Textbook Exercises

The explanations for the textbook activities are self-explanatory. Check students for use of active voice and other broadcast style.

1. Broadcast brief

This is a very basic hard-news brief. Check to make sure students have used active voice. Here is an example for comparative purposes.

A CONSUMER ACTION GROUP IS CHARGING TONIGHT THAT THE PUBLIX GROCERY STORE CHAIN IS GUILTY OF DISCRIMINATION. THE FLORIDA CONSUMER'S FEDERATION SAYS PUBLIX HAS FAILED TO PUT ENOUGH WOMEN, BLACKS AND HISPANICS IN MANAGEMENT JOBS. IT ALSO COMPLAINS THAT THE COMPANY DOESN'T HAVE ENOUGH STORES IN MINORITY NEIGHBORHOODS. PUBLIX PRESIDENT MARK HOLLIS ADMITS TO SHORTCOMINGS, BUT SAYS IT IS WORKING HARD TO OVERCOME THEM.

2. Louisville chase

This is an interesting story, but the writer can't get too wrapped up in telling it for television, because typically the station will have no pictures or relatively static aftermath pictures that don't help tell the story. Here are two versions. One is fairly straightforward, with a direct lead. The other uses an indirect lead and is a little longer but probably gets the story across to the audience better.

A 16-YEAR OLD BOY LED POLICE ON A HIGH-SPEED CAR CHASE THROUGH A SECTION OF TOWN CROWDED WITH PEDESTRIANS. POLICE ARE NOT RELEASING THE NAME OF THE DRIVER, WHO IS 16 YEARS OLD. THE CHASE STARTED WHEN A POLICE OFFICER SAW THE CAR THE BOY WAS DRIVING RUN OVER A STOP SIGN. THAT STARTED AN 80-MILE-AN-HOUR CHASE THROUGH THE HIGHLAND SECTION OF TOWN, PAST SIDEWALKS

CROWDED WITH PEDESTRIANS. THE BOY FACES CHARGES INCLUDING WANTON ENDANGERMENT.

- 30 -

WHEN OFFICER JOHN BUTTS SAW A CAR RUN OVER A STOP SIGN, HE TRIED TO PULL IT OVER.   THE CAR SPED OFF, FORCED OTHER CARS OFF THE ROAD, AND NARROWLY MISSED SEVERAL PEDESTRIANS IN THE HIGHLANDS SECTION OF LOUISVILLE. THE CHASE FINALLY ENDED WHEN THE VEHICLE REAR-ENDED BUTTS' PATROL CAR. POLICE WILL NOT RELEASE THE NAME OF THE DRIVER.   IT SEEMS HE WAS 16 YEARS OLD. . . AND DRIVING WITHOUT A LICENSE. THAT MAY BE THE LEAST OF HIS PROBLEMS, BECAUSE HE FACES CHARGES OF WANTON ENDANGERMENT AND RESISTING ARREST.

- 30 -

3 to 5. Newscasts and teasers

If possible, get scripts from your local television news station so students can see models, especially a rundown of the news show.

Workbook Exercises

13-1. Church embezzler

The focus of this story should be on the *sentencing*, because that's the most recent element in the story. Anything else is old information, and might lose the interest of viewers familiar with the story. From there, we can tell the story of the embezzlement. Here are some other points to check in this exercise:
- The lead must be brief and interesting.
- The writer must be careful to keep this story tightly focused on the interesting elements of the case, not details that will be less meaningful to the viewer. A good broadcast writer will not generally use the street address of the church, the exact name of the court in which the case was tried, or the judge's name in a story like this, unless there's a

specific reason for using the detail. The writer has one more reason to keep this story short: It has no visuals.

- Watch for the way numbers are written in the story (e.g., 10-thousanddollars). Normally the man's age would read "26-year-old," unless the expression comes at the start of a sentence. Avoid the awkward phrase "the 26-year-old Poteet" where his age substitutes for his first name.
- The use of the word "monies" in the notes is a bit of a trap. "Money" is the correct word to use in this case.

Police stories and court cases often contain too many passive verbs. Don't let writers fall into the trap of using too many expressions such as "Poteet's embezzlement was discovered by another employee" and "A church employee was sentenced today." This example has no passive voice it.

AN OVERLAND PARK MAN FACES THREE YEARS IN PRISON FOR TAKING

HIS <u>OWN</u> COLLECTION AT A LOCAL CHURCH. TWENTY-SIX-YEAR-OLD RON

POTEET POCKETED ABOUT 70-THOUSAND DOLLARS FROM COLLECTIONS

AT PRESBYTERIAN FELLOWSHIP CHURCH IN OVERLAND PARK. ANOTHER

CHURCH EMPLOYEE DISCOVERED THAT POTEET WAS TAKING MONEY OUT

OF COLLECTION ENVELOPES. EARLIER POTEET PLEADED GUILTY TO

EMBEZZLEMENT. TODAY A DISTRICT COURT JUDGE SENTENCED POTEET

TO THREE YEARS AND A 10-THOUSAND DOLLAR FINE.

–30–

Here is a shorter version of the same story that still will get the point across; TV news is always looking for brevity:

A FORMER CHURCH EMPLOYEE FACES A PRISON SENTENCE FOR

EMBEZZLING CHURCH DONATIONS. THE EMPLOYEE, 26-YEAR-OLD RON

POTEET, ADMITTED HE TOOK ABOUT 70-THOUSAND DOLLARS FROM

PRESBYTERIAN FELLOWSHIP CHURCH IN OVERLAND PARK. TODAY POTEET

RECEIVED A   THREE-YEAR PRISON SENTENCE AND   A 10-THOUSAND

DOLLAR FINE.

-- 30 --

Sometimes information is incomplete or confusing in wire stories, as is the case here. The fire actually destroyed three buildings, two at the lumberyard *and* the old railroad station, but that isn't easy to tell from the wire.

The writer must be careful not to go overboard by including information that will not be of interest to the viewing audience. The items about where the investigators' meeting will take place and who will take part fall into the "who cares?" category.

Broadcast stories avoid "last night" leads – especially by 6:00 the next night. The lead should contain a new element to maintain the freshness of the story and the newscast as a whole. The "last night" element can come later in the story. Avoid the lead, "A lumberyard in Delton was destroyed by fire last night." It's both passive and dated. The lead sentence on-camera should be brief. We want to get to the video of the fire, not look at the anchor.

The newest elements are the owner's problems staying in business and the investigation. The owner probably makes a more interesting and human angle for the lead than the investigation – but that's a story-to-story decision writers have to make. Make sure to write out the word "company," if used, and avoid abbreviations in general. It's also more conversational to say "8:30 last night" than "8:30 P.M." The actual script would be double-spaced.

LUMBER FIRE

VO LEAD-IN	LORI	THE OWNER OF A CHARRED LUMBERYARD IN DELTON IS TRYING TO GET BACK INTO BUSINESS.
TAKE VO		THE DELTON LUMBER COMPANY SUFFERED HEAVY DAMAGE LAST NIGHT IN A FIRE.
		THE FIRE DESTROYED THREE BUILDINGS INCLUDING THE FORMER DELTON RAILROAD DEPOT.
SUPER: DELTON		IT BURNED OUT OF CONTROL FOR TWO AND A-HALF HOURS AND DID AROUND 200-THOUSAND DOLLARS DAMAGE.
SUPER: LAST NIGHT		THE YARD'S OWNER SAYS HE'LL TRY TO GET RIGHT BACK INTO BUSINESS IN SPITE OF THE DAMAGE BECAUSE HIS CUSTOMERS ARE DEPENDING ON HIM FOR LUMBER.

--30--

13-3. Acid arrests

This is a multi-element story, typical of local TV-news packages. A good organization is effect (acid arrests) and cause (probable local manufacturer). Closing the story by saying police would like to catch up with the drug's maker is a strong way of indicating where the story is headed or what is the possible solution to the problem.

The available visuals also affect the organization of TV packages. In this case, it's probably strongest to begin with the video of the drugs. While the young users are good "humanization" to the story, we apparently weren't given access to them for interviews, which softens their impact (and might give students some ideas for doing follow-up stories).

If you give a story like this to five professional writers, they'll come up with five different ways of handling it. Some will be better than others, but there's no single correct way. Here is one version, printed here in single spacing but should be double spaced for actual script:

ACID Date PKG LEAD-IN	RANDALL	A POPULAR – AND DANGEROUS – DRUG FROM THE SIXTIES IS MAKING A COMEBACK. PHIL MOORE REPORTS ON THE INVASION OF THE DRUG KNOWN AS ACID.
TAKE PKG		
		BAG AFTER BAG OF DRUGS IN THIS EVIDENCE ROOM TESTIFY THAT L–S–D IS BACK.
SUPER: KANSAS CITYDRUG ENFORCEMENT ADMIN.		SO DO THE ARREST FIGURES IN NORTHEAST KANSAS – ARRESTS HAVE INCREASED FROM THREE LAST YEAR TO 10 THIS YEAR. THE HEAD OF THE KANSAS CITY OFFICE OF THE DRUG ENFORCEMENT ADMINISTRATION SAYS HE KNOWS WHY.
SUPER: OTTO PRIVETTE DRUG ENFORCEMENT AGENT		------------------------------------ (BITE:12) IN: "MORE PEOPLE ARE USING. . ." OUT: ". . .ON THE PROBLEM." ------------------------------------

SUPER:LAWRENCE

AND MANY OF THOSE ARRESTED WILL PROBABLY BE TEENAGERS, LIKE THE YOUNG PEOPLE LYNNE HARRIS IS COUNSELING AT THIS SESSION IN LAWRENCE.

HARRIS SAYS THE DRUG APPEALS TO TEENAGERS IN PART BECAUSE ITS EFFECTS LAST A LONG TIME. BUT BUYERS MAY BE GETTING INTO SOMETHING EVEN MORE DANGEROUS THAN THE L-S-D ITSELF.

SUPER: LYNNE HARRIS DRUG COUNSELOR

BITE: (:10)
IN: "A LOT OF THE L-S-D
OUT: "...IT'S DOUBLY DANGEROUS."

THE STRYCHNINE IS SUPPOSED TO ENHANCE THE EFFECTS OF L-S-D, BUT IT CAN ALSO POISON THE USER.

THAT HAS POLICE LOOKING FOR THE SOURCE. THEY MAYNOT HAVE TO LOOK FAR, BECAUSE THEY SAY SOMEBODY IN THIS REGION MAY BE TURNING OUT THE DRUG. AND POLICE SAY THEY'D LIKE TO CATCH THAT MANUFACTURER.

PHIL MOORE REPORTING.

--30--

13-4. Simplify words

Here are some suggestions:

1. utilize: use
2. interrogate: question
3. purchase: buy
4. necessitate: need
5. deceased: dead
6. terminate:end
7. contribute: give
8. perpetrator: suspect
9. apprehended: arrest
10. incarcerated: jailed

13-5. Rewrite sentences in active voice

Here are some suggested changes:

1. Safeway may purchase the Carrs food chain.
2. Fire destroyed two apartment houses on the east side of town this morning.
3. Many professors consider addiction to the Internet a growing problem among college students.
4. Psychiatrists offer several reasons for the appeal of the Internet to college students.
5. An accident occurs almost every month at the intersection of Northern Lights Boulevard and Bragaw Street.
6. Fire destroyed at least 30 hillside homes.
7. Several students will drop out of school if tuition is increased.
8. Police shot an Anchorage man after they discovered that he killed a moose.
9. Two students won the lottery.
10. Police think the suspect who drove the getaway car was involved in several other robberies.

13-6. Brief news (Write a 15-second spot)

This is a bit easier because it is just an announcement. Make sure students include the time and place as well as mention of a film and forum. If students use "habeas corpus" relief, ask them to define it. That's built into this assignment to force students to think. Most viewers would not understand the term so it should not be used. However, many students will automatically include it even if they don't understand it.

13-7. News Feature

This is a challenging exercise because of the limited space. Students may use a hard or soft lead such as the one on the release. The concepts to include are the idea that prayer may be good for your health and that studies confirm links between lower blood pressure and heart rates and prayer. It is also important to include the researcher, Tim Daaleman and his grant.

Web Writing

14

Goals

- To teach students to think creatively about planning and writing packages designed for the Web.
- To give students practice in writing personal journalism for the Web.
- To give students practice in writing headlines and summary blurbs to entice readers into their online stories.
- To give students practice in using style geared to Web readability.

Throughout the textbook online coach boxes have been offered to encourage students to begin thinking about writing online versions of their news stories. As more news organizations adopt the idea of convergence, students will need to be skilled in various media. This chapter gives students a chance to gain skills in writing for the Web.

Teaching Suggestions

Before students can write well for the Web, they should read online. I begin this chapter and my online journalism course by asking students to analyze the difference between online and print writing. Often their local print and online newspaper sites do not reflect any differences so we discuss whether they should. I also direct students to packages designed specifically for the Web such as those at CNN.com or MSNBC.com. We discuss qualities of Web writing such as interactivity, multimedia, links, different versions – brief, longer and in-depth – and what they like or dislike about reading online. Then we practice various forms of online writing. I encourage students to suggest new forms of writing because the Web is a young medium that is constantly changing and offers opportunities for innovation.

Textbook Exercises

1. Headlines and blurbs

If the headline and summary blurb don't entice the reader into the story, it doesn't matter how well the story is written. Readers have to click first. Unlike print media where readers can scan a page, a Web page usually offers many choices – often just headlines. As a result, training students to think of headlines and summary blurbs is a good way to help them focus their stories and promote them. An easy way to do this is to use the local or campus newspaper. Sometimes the headlines will convert well to the Web but often they do not.

2. Personal Essay

This is the first major writing assignment I give in Web writing and in my online journalism class because it helps students think creatively and differently for the Web. Personal journalism thrives on the Web, but this type of writing is usually a departure from the news writing students have learned. I use *www.fray.com* and *www.journale.com* for inspiration. This assignment works well if you ask students to write about a traumatic experience they have had, a memorable experience, a childhood memory or experience that may have been fun for them.

This is usually hard for students at first, but my students liked this assignment the best. One student wrote about his trip to Mexico and his fear of scorpions. Another wrote about her battle with cancer.

This assignment works best if you ask students to design their stories as chunks (one or two screens per chunk) with cliffhangers at the end of each chunk to entice readers to click into the next part. Also ask them to add an interactive element such as a question: Have you ever had a frightening experience or similar question. This helps students think interactively, a major element of Web writing.

3. Interviews – 1 cent

This exercise was inspired by a site, Interviews: 50 cents, on the Journal E Web site previously mentioned. I loved the idea and adapted it for the class.

Another adaptation of this idea was a project we did for Thanksgiving. Students conducted interviews with people about their favorite Thanksgiving memories and we created a package with brief vignettes for the online campus newspaper.

4. Converting a story for the Web

This exercise is intended to help students think how online writing should differ from print. Encourage them to provide links, interactive elements and plan a storyboard to decide if a news story in the newspaper or one they have written should have more or different elements for the Web.

5. Web story

The key elements to look for in rewriting this story are lists (especially for the statistical information), boldfaced subheads and interactivity such as a poll, questions or at the very least, links. Students may be able to link to the original story, which was on the Web site for the Centers for Disease Control, although that link may have disappeared.

Workbook Exercises

14-1. Plan a Web project

The main point of this exercise is to encourage students' creativity. If they don't have to create the package, they can be as innovative as they wish without worrying about whether they have the software for multimedia or other technical drawbacks. This works best if you put students in small groups to plan a project they choose or one you assign. Then let each group discuss their storyboards.

14-2. Headlines and blurbs

Students will find this exercise more challenging if you limit the number of words they may write in their headlines. Most of these examples were adapted from Associated Press stories, which had headlines of fewer than six words. Students' headlines and blurbs may be far more creative than these, but here are some AP examples:

a. **Body of missing biologist found**

A body of a Harvard University professor who disappeared more than a month ago was found Saturday in the Mississippi River at Vidalia, La.

b. **Custodian teaching science at school**

The new high school science teacher came to class wearing coveralls and boots, the uniform he wore just the day before as the school's janitor.

c. Washington law targets inattentive drivers

Drivers who talk on cell phones, put on makeup or otherwise don't watch the roads in North Bend, Wash., will soon face stiffer penalties for moving violations.

d. Montana worries about drinking deaths

People in Montana are more likely to die in alcohol-related crashes than motorists in almost any other state.

e. Web site lets cats catch birds with mouse

Cats who like to chase moving objects on a computer can now use a mouse on their very own Web site.

14-3. Web briefs

Here are some students' versions:

a. Study: Dogs with short noses risk lung cancer

Dogs with short noses are 50 percent more likely to develop lung cancer when they live with owners who smoke, according to a Colorado State University study on environmental health.

A long nose may be a dog's best defense against second-hand smoke. A Colorado State University found that long-nosed dogs, such as collies and retrievers, were less likely to contract lung cancer from contact with smoke.

b. Write a two-paragraph brief based on the following information.

Florida is the Sunshine State, and Professor Lee Stefanakos of the University of South Florida is taking advantage of it. He is operating the country's first solar-powered vehicle.

With a $1 million grant from the U.S. Department of energy, Stefanakos came up with a car that costs 4 cents per mile to run with solar energy instead of 40 cents a mile for gas-powered cars. The car has solar panels mounted on the roof and can go up to 60 miles on a charge. And, of course, it is equipped with air conditioning.

14-4. Chunk-style writing with cliffhangers

Here is the original story, written for print, but adapted here for the Web. Any of these chunks may be combined.

If you want an intro page, you could write the first chunk as follows with this cliffhanger ending:

When a skunk wandered through the open door of National Furniture Liquidators on Monday afternoon, three strong and brave employees did what anyone would do.

They hid.

"If it would have been a squirrel, I would have chased him out with a broom," said acting assistant manager Dennis Goke.

But it wasn't a squirrel. It was something more powerful – or, at least, something with a more powerful weapon.

Chunk 2

With thousands of dollars worth of overstuffed chairs, sofas and love seats at stake, Goke wasn't taking any chances. So for the first hour, the skunk was allowed the run of the place, which is at 1202 Maple Grove Road. It wandered up and down the warehouse aisles while employees eyeballed it warily from the doorway.

At one point, they tried to lure it out with a trail of whole wheat bread crumbs, but the skunk wasn't hungry. (The crumbs did attract dozens of gulls, though, which screeched and screamed and flapped and gorged until most of the bread was gone.)

Shortly after Rich Ulkus of Animal Allies arrived to see what he could do, the skunk had had enough. There were too many people around and too much commotion. It disappeared into hiding somewhere in the bowels of the store.

Chunk 3

That made employees more nervous than watching it roam the aisles.

Ulkus spent a few minutes on his hands and knees, shining a floodlight under some of the couches and drawing gasps of admiration and comments about his bravery from the others, but he couldn't find the skunk.

So he and Goke baited a trap with tuna, wrapped the whole thing in a blanket and stuck it in a corner. (Wondering as they did so how, exactly, they were to remove the trap once the skunk was inside it.)

Although the employees stayed outside more than in, the store didn't close. Business continued throughout the afternoon, if not exactly business as usual.

As customers pulled into the parking lot, they were greeted by the unsettling warning of "Hey, we got a loose skunk in here!"

Store manager Bill Frolichman, who had been on vacation, arrived late in the afternoon to oversee the situation. He decided to wait until closing, then try to spook out the skunk with bright lights and rock music.

Chunk 4

"I've worked in strange situations before," he said. "I've worked in floods. I've worked without any power in the building."

Brave talk, though none of those circumstances had the opportunity to wreak quite as much havoc as a skunk.

Still, Frolichman was as good as his word. By 8 p.m., the store was closed and the music was playing – but the skunk remained at large.

Laurie Hertzel, *The* (Duluth) *News-Tribune*. Reprinted with permission.

14-5. Web news story

 The main point here is to put the statistics in list form.

A new study claims that about 3 percent of college women are victims of rape or attempted rape during a college year. The study, released today by the U.S. Department of Justice's National Institute of Justice and the Bureau of Justice Statistics, also estimated that about 13 percent of college woman have been stalked since the beginning of the school year.

The report, "The Sexual Victimization of College Women," offers a comprehensive look into the prevalence and nature of sexual assault occurring at American colleges. The federally funded study was conducted by Bonnie S. Fisher, a professor at the University of Cincinnati.

Number of incidents

Of the incidents of sexual victimization, the vast majority occurred after 6 p.m. in living quarters. For completed rapes, the study revealed:

- Nearly 60 percent that took place on campus occurred in the victim's residence
- 31 percent occurred in other living quarters on campus
- 10 percent occurred at a fraternity.

Most off-campus victimization, especially rapes, also occurred in residences. However, particularly for sexual contacts and threatened victimizations, incidents also took place in bars, dance clubs, nightclubs and work settings. Most of the sexually assaulted women knew the person who victimized them.

Defining rape

Based on their findings, Bonnie Fisher and her colleagues estimate that the women at a college that has 10,000 female students could experience more than 350 rapes a year-- a finding with serious policy implications for college administrators. Fisher also found that many women do not characterize their sexual victimizations as a crime for a number of reasons (such as embarrassment, not clearly understanding the legal definition of rape, or not wanting to define someone they know who victimized them as a rapist) or because they blame themselves for their sexual assault. The study reinforces the importance of many organizations' efforts to improve education and knowledge about sexual assault.

Previous research suggests that these women are at greater risk for rape and other forms of sexual assault than women in the general population or in a comparable age group.

NCWSV study results are based on a telephone survey of a randomly selected, national sample of 4,446 women who were attending a 2- or 4-year college or university. The sample was limited to schools with at least 1,000 students.

Put these links at the end:

Department of Justice Web site: *http://www.ojp.usdoj.gov/nij/*.

Office of Justice home page at *http://www.ojp.usdoj.gov*.

Accuracy and Libel 15

Goals

- To make students aware of the importance of accuracy
- To give students a basic understanding of libel and invasion of privacy
- To discuss accuracy and libel problems created on the Internet

Teaching Suggestions

This chapter can be taught at any time during the course, but it is particularly effective when taught just before or concurrently with Chapter 22, Crime and Punishment.

Students need to understand that inaccuracy is a very serious offense. Although I do not give grades on papers because I use the portfolio method explained in the preface, I make an exception for inaccuracy. I state in my syllabus that any factual inaccuracy, including a misspelled name, will result in an automatic F. On occasion, I will put a dollar amount on a paper, saying this paper is worth $50,000 – the cost of the lawsuit – or another sum if it contains libelous information. Even though students have a chance to correct their errors in the rewriting phase, the original paper still counts against their final grade. I think the automatic failure policy reinforces the need for accuracy. In conjunction with discussions about accuracy, you can also discuss ethics and the need for fairness.

The Internet is creating several new concerns about accuracy and libel. In addition, plagiarism has become rampant because of easy access to information. Ask students to raise some of their concerns about new issues – especially accuracy of Internet sources – created by online information. Check the Web site for this book for many related resources: *http://info.wadsworth.com/rich*.

Textbook Exercises

1. Corrections

You can use your local newspaper, if it has a corrections policy, or a national newspaper. If students check corrections for a few days or a week, they will get an idea of the most common mistakes. This may also be a good activity to combine with a discussion of libel, reinforcing that corrections do not prevent libel suits.

As an alternative to this exercise or a supplemental one, you could assign each student to interview one or two editors in the area about their corrections policies and ask editors how seriously they view inaccuracy at their publications.

2. Actual malice

This is a hard concept for many students to understand. They should explain this means publishing information knowing that it was false or with "reckless disregard" for whether it was false.

3. Libel

This situation is based on the case of former Sen. Brock Adams, D-Wash., who was accused of sexual harassment and sexual abuse by eight women. *The Seattle Times* published their accusations but not their names. Adams denied the accusations but withdrew from his re-election campaign the day the article was published. Accompanying the article was a message to readers from Michael Fancher, editor of *The Seattle Times,* in which he explained why the newspaper was breaking its policy prohibiting use of anonymous sources. He said the newspaper had been investigating allegations against the senator for three-and-a half years, and it became clear that sources would not go on the record. He said that because the newspaper felt the women's charges reflected directly on the senator's fitness for office, the paper decided to publish their allegations, which the women revealed on the ground that their names be withheld. However, the *Times* did get seven of the women to agree to testify in court if Adams sued.

This case also represents an ethical dilemma and can generate some good discussion in class. Reaction to the *Times* decision was mixed. Discuss whether students think the newspaper did the right thing, whether it was worth the risk of libel, when should you use anonymous sources, and what they would have done if they had been the editor.

During the scandal and subsequent impeachment of President Clinton, several politicians were "outed" or exposed for their extramarital sexual relationships. Discuss whether the sexual relationships of politicians will continue to pose ethical dilemmas for the media.

4. Privacy #1

This issue could be an invasion of privacy, but only a court would really determine that. Some issues for discussion: Unlike the Cox Broadcasting case, the hospital records are not public record. However, the candidate is a public figure, so his background can be considered of "legitimate public concern." Ask students to weigh the criteria for determining public disclosure of private facts.

5. Privacy #2

This exercise is based on *Daily Times Democrat v. Graham,* a Georgia case in which Flora Bell Graham sued the newspaper because it printed a photograph that she claimed invaded her privacy by disclosing an embarrassing fact. The picture revealed her underwear as her skirt blew up to her shoulders when she emerged from the fun house at a county fair. Discuss these elements with students: The photograph was taken on public property. Was the photographer within his rights to shoot it? The newspaper argued that the photographer had the right to shoot the picture in a public place and that it was newsworthy. But the Georgia Supreme Court upheld a lower court decision that found that Graham's underwear was not newsworthy and it was exposed against her will.

6. Search the Internet

Students should be learn how to use the Internet to search for legal documents. They can link to them directly from the Web site for this book. Encourage students to browse through Findlaw and other sites linked to the textbook Web site. The site, Cyberspace Law for Non-Lawyers, contains an excellent, clear explanation of libel and other laws in online media.

Workbook Exercises

15-1. Libel quiz

The two libel exercises and the discussion were devised by Tom Volek, media law professor at the University of Kansas. Here are the correct answers.

1. a. Truth **Rationale:** Ultimately, truth is the best defense because libel is by definition "false and defamatory." If you remove the element of falsity, it's not libelous. When a reporter relies only on Sullivan or privilege, he or she has published something false and defamatory and is, in essence, falling back on a "technical" defense. A columnist or editorial writer's opinion must rely on "facts truly stated or commonly known" to qualify for protection under "fair comment and criticism. "

2. d. That the reporter made a false statement either knowing the information was wrong, or with reckless disregard for whether it was wrong or not. **Rationale:** "Actual malice" is a legal term that indicates that the reporter either knew that information was wrong before she or he published it or exercised extremely poor judgment about whether it was wrong. Honest efforts to find and reach multiple sources, check facts and write stories in a fair and balanced way will prevent a finding of "actual malice."

3. b. With public figure or public official plaintiffs. **Rationale:** Public figures and public officials have to prove actual malice before collecting damages from the press. Private figures only have to prove "negligence" to recover damages from the press. "Negligence" may be thought of as carelessness.

4. d. In recognition that in a democracy, private figures, too, have to be ready for sharp or unpleasant attacks in the press. **Rationale:** The foundation of the Sullivan holding was the protection of the press from public officials by forcing those public officials to prove actual malice, even if the press published something false about the officials. This encourages more aggressive press coverage of public issues because it gives the press protection even if it makes a false statement, as long as the press tries to report the truth. Conversely, private people have more protection from the press. If a newspaper prints something false and defamatory about a private person, that person only has to prove negligence to recover damages.

5. c. You may print defamatory statements from a public proceeding or public record as long as you are being fair and accurate. *Rationale:* "Privilege" is a legal term, facilitating the exchange in information in certain, protected situations. Court trials require people to speak their minds freely, even though accusations and evidence may indeed be defamatory and perhaps even false. Thus court participants are "absolutely privileged" from libel suits arising from their participation. The press, as a surrogate for the public, has a "qualified privilege" to report these situations as long as it does so fairly and accurately.

6. a. You may be guilty of invasion of privacy under the intrusion category.
Rationale: You may only take pictures (or report) from a public place (like a sidewalk) "seeing what the unaided eye can see, hearing what the unaided ear can hear." This situation clearly could lead to an invasion of privacy lawsuit, which the reporter could lose. A public place (like a sidewalk) is not the same as a public record or an official recording of public business, like a court record or land records.

7. c. The ad people have to receive his permission and pay him if he requests it, since this is for commercial purposes. *Rationale:* The use of a person's name, likeness, persona, photograph or voice for commercial purposes requires her or his permission. If the person wants to be paid, you must negotiate a contract with them. If that person wants more money than you are willing to pay, you may not use her or him. Unless you have a person's consent, the only other defense you have is newsworthiness, which is ordinarily not a defense for commercial speech.

8. a. You took the information from a public record. *Rationale:* Taking information from the public record is a very strong defense in this category of invasion of privacy. Again, the courts have held that the press is a surrogate for the public, and public records ordinarily are open to inspection by anyone.

9. c. Check details, even little things, to see if a source or story "doesn't add up. *Rationale:* There is no such thing as an acceptable level of inaccuracy. Even small inaccuracies hurt the reporter's credibility. At the worst, they can lead to a lawsuit. The best reporters check everything in a story. They see if the minute details "add up." If these reporters find inconsistencies or inaccuracies in their information, they try to sort out the truth. If they suspect a source may be lying or not telling the whole truth, they don't use the source.

10. d. Is a way that some journalists catch inaccuracies before publication. *Rationale:* Although some editors don't like pre-publication reviews by sources, many experienced journalists find that such reviews help them improve accuracy. The reporters make it clear to the sources that the source only has the right to check accuracy, not to change the story.

15-2. Libel quiz #2

1. Libel is a published defamation; slander is oral defamation.
2. Pervasive, limited or vortex, and involuntary. Pervasive is a person who has gained prominence – celebrities. Vortex or limited is one who voluntary entered a public controversy to influence the outcome. Involuntary is someone thrust into a public controversy against his or her will.
3. Hutchinson did not willingly enter public controversy and did not have regular and continuing access to the media.
4. Falsity, damage to his or her reputation and that the material was published with actual malice, knowledge that it was false or disregard for the facts.
5. A public official must prove actual malice; private people may only have to prove negligence in some states.
6. Public officials have complete immunity against libel to make statements in the course of their official duties.
7. You can print defamatory statements by public officials if you are fair and accurate and if the information is from a public proceeding or public record.
8. Physical or mental intrusion into a person's solitude, public disclosure of private facts, false light, and use of a person's name without his or her permission.
9. Because reporters used subterfuge to gain the information and invaded his privacy.
10. The purpose of the act is to provide a consistent law throughout the country. The publication must run a full, fair, and timely correction.

15-3. Online legal issues

1. **False.** The U.S. Supreme Court ruled in Zeran v. AOL that the Internet Service Provider is not responsible for messages posted by a third party.
2. **False.**
3. **False.** The U.S. Supreme Court ruled that only those portions of the Communications Decency Act of 1996 that would limit distribution of indecent material to minors were unconstitutional.
4. **True**
5. **False**
6. **True**
7. **False**
8. **False.** If a site is encrypted, that means it contains special codes that only people authorized by the site can read.
9. **True**
10. **False**

15-4. Legal scenarios

This exercise lends itself well to class discussion, especially if you put students in small groups. You can also use it as a written exercise.

1. School board meeting. The comments were made during the public meeting; therefore you are legally entitled to use them. However, this is more of an ethical issue. You may be safer to hold the information until you have more evidence. But either way, you should ask yourself several questions before deciding to use this material. For example:
    - How many guidance counselors are there in this town? If you only one, you identify that person even without his or her name. If only two, both are hurt by the accusations, which may be false.
    - Who is this member of the audience and how credible is this person?
    - Is there any evidence that can be checked or substantiated to this person's allegations.
    - What harm or benefit is there in publishing this material?
2. **Officer's comments:** They are not libelous if the officer accuses the man of being rapist and that is on the public record. If he or she says this to you privately, the information could be libelous.
3. **Council member's comments:** No, the member does not have absolute privilege because the comments were not made in a public meeting.
4. **Roaches:** Yes, you can always be sued. If you have factual evidence that roaches crawled across the table, you can say that.
5. **Tasteless food:** You are protected because this is an opinion column.
6. **Private property:** Yes. You can only photograph or use what the unaided eye can see or ear can hear.
7. **Medical records:** Yes, this is an invasion of privacy because medical records are not public records.
8. **Michael Jordon photo:** Not without his permission. This is a violation of his privacy and his rights to use his image for commercial purposes without permission.
9. **Plagiarism:** Yes, this can be considered plagiarism, especially if you copy the comments and don't attribute them. It is unlikely to be considered fair use, which is more often based on how much of the material you use and for what purpose. Educational purposes are favored.
10. **Discussion group libel:** Yes, you can sue, but the Internet service provider is probably not at fault. The U.S. Supreme Court ruled in one case (Zeran v. AOL) that the Internet service provider is not responsible for messages posted by a third party.

Ethics

16

Goals

- To make students aware of ethical issues in the media
- To teach students moral reasoning concepts
- To make students aware of media codes of ethics
- To help students become aware of emerging online ethical issues

This chapter can be taught at any point during the course. It is preferable, however, to discuss ethical issues as they arise either in connection with stories the students are writing or local and national news stories. This new edition of the textbook attempts to do that with the inclusion of several ethical dilemmas throughout the book. However, other ethical problems can be discussed related to the chapters you are using. Students enjoy discussing ethical issues, and the cases usually provide stimulating discussion. Ask students to bring in other cases or situations that they consider to be ethical problems they have read in the newspaper or watched on TV news.

The Internet is creating several new ethical dilemmas as well. Ask students to raise some of their concerns about privacy, ethics of quoting from Internet sources and other emerging issues. Check the Web site for this book for many online resources: *http://info.wadsworth.com/rich.*

Teaching Suggestions

To encourage discussion among all students, consider splitting the class into small groups. Then have each group debate the cases and present its views. Before teaching some of the moral reasoning methods, ask students to define their values as journalists. Values such as accuracy, fairness, helpfulness (to serve the public) and others can be used as guiding principles.

When you first present a case, ask students to express their gut reaction. Then ask them to see if they can justify their initial decision by using some of the moral reasoning methods. One method I have found helpful is role-playing. Ask students to assume various roles of all the stakeholders – people who will be affected by the story. After students have expressed their gut reactions, ask them to argue the opposite point of view and then decide if they can still justify their initial decision.

On other occasions I will ask students to write an editor's note to readers or viewers explaining their decision, or I ask them to assume that they have to explain their rationale to the person most upset by the story. In all cases, we define the dilemma, discuss alternatives and the effect on various stakeholders and then justify the decision.

Encourage students to argue and feel free to disagree. In most of the cases presented in the textbook and workbook, editors and media critics disagreed about the outcome.

Textbook Exercises

1. Moral reasoning

a. Anonymous source/rumors about senator's homosexuality: This case raises issues of privacy as well as anonymous sources. When is a politician's sex life a relevant issue? You might discuss whether the media should have revealed allegations by Gennifer Flowers, who claimed she had an affair with President Clinton prior to his election. Because the media backlash was so much greater in this case than in the Gary Hart case, you could ask students what they think will happen in future presidential election campaigns.

b. The public reaction to the Arthur Ashe case created even more media backlash. This case also raises the question of anonymous sources – although *USA Today* stuck by its policy of not revealing that Ashe had AIDS until it could be confirmed by a source on the record. Students generally are opposed to revealing Ashe's condition on the grounds that he was entitled to his privacy and he was no longer a practicing athlete. However, before Ashe died on Feb. 6, 1993, almost a year after he felt forced to reveal his condition, he had become a spokesman for the disease and had said he was surprised by the outpouring of warmth and understanding he had received from so many people. That may affect how students respond to this issue. You could ask them how they would deal with the same issue if it affected another prominent athlete today.

c. The nursing home case involves deception, and students usually favor the technique if they feel it will help the public. Ask them to explore all alternatives before they use this technique.

2. Student government candidate

This case should provoke some interesting discussion. Ask the students to justify their reasoning using relevance, accuracy, truth and issues they may raise. Other discussion questions: How important was timing? If you had learned of the criminal background after the candidate had resigned, would you have printed it? To complicate the issue, the reporter who checked the candidate's police records was a close friend of the candidate's running mate. Discuss how students would feel about hurting their friend or if they think they would have a conflict of interest in this case.

3. Anti-holocaust advertisement

This should provoke interesting discussion. You could invite a member from Hillel or the Jewish community to class for this. Students at Kennesaw State College in Georgia refused to print the advertisement, as did many other campus newspapers, because they thought it would be too offensive. However, others decided to print the ad and suffered backlash from the university and local communities. To add a modern twist to the dilemma, ask students if they would link to an online site that espouses anti-semitic philosophy.

4. Online pornography

Again in this exercise, discuss with students whether they would link to pornographic sites. If the campus newspaper receives university funding, especially if this is a state-funded institution, how will that affect students' decisions? Several universities have experienced opposition from community organizations for providing links or newsgroups that offer pornography.

Workbook Exercises

The workbook exercises are based on real cases from *The Hartford Courant* and were provided by Henry McNulty, the newspaper's former reader representative, who was one of the leading ombudsmen in the country. I chose them because they can give students some idea of the problems editors face on a daily basis and how readers feel about these decisions. Ask students to discuss the cases, and then distribute the results of the informal surveys that McNulty conducted so students can compare their reactions with those of readers and editors.

16-1. The bad joke

- ❏ You delete the joke, because you consider it inappropriate for your newspaper.
  Readers 33%   Editors 11%
- ❏ You let it stand, on the grounds that otherwise your readers can't properly judge the actions of the politician and those people who walked out.
  Readers 67%   Editors 89%

McNulty's remarks: Two thirds of the readers said that in such a case it's appropriate to show exactly what all the fuss was about. "Let the readers decide if it was offensive or just an excuse for some group to stage a walkout," said one reader. "The joke will become public knowledge very soon anyway," another reader added.

But one-third of the respondents disagreed. "There is no advantage to including an off-color joke in the newspaper," a reader said. "It just might be too offensive."

Almost 90 percent of the editors would allow it. I (McNulty) go along with them and the majority of readers – as long as the language isn't too raw. Then a paraphrase might be in order.

16-2. The telephone number

- ❏ You let the phone number stand.
  Readers 53%   Editors 32%
- ❏ You delete the phone number.
  Readers 47%   Editors 68%

McNulty's remarks: This case resulted in the closest reader vote. "Interested parties would call your paper asking for more information or the number if you didn't print it," said one high school journalism teacher. "You are not promoting abortion by providing phone numbers," the teacher added. But among the 47 percent who said no were these comments: "If usually such numbers are not included in news stories, fairness is the key here," wrote a professor from Central Connecticut State University.
A number of those voting no said they are pro-choice, but they thought printing this number would be unfair. I'm very much in favor of adding all sorts of useful information (such as phone numbers and addresses) to news stories, but only if it's done fairly and consistently. In this case, the newspaper had failed to do the same for an anti-abortion group. So reluctantly, I'd vote with the minority of readers and leave out the number.

16-3. Son of superintendent

     ❑ You leave in the mention of the father, because you believe this fact is important to your readers.

        Readers   39%   Editors 68%

     ❑ You delete the reference to the father.

        Readers   61%   Editors 32%

McNulty's remarks: This case presented a frequent newsroom dilemma. A young man is arrested; his father is a well-known town official. Should the father be mentioned, for identification purposes, in the story of the son's arrest? Readers and editors were at odds in this case. "The problem is with the son," said one reader.

I'm afraid the editors will be in hot water no matter which way the decision goes. If the father's name is used, many readers will say the newspaper is insensitive and unfair. If it isn't used, there are likely to be allegations of a cover-up. If it were up to me, I'd report the family connection in most cases. Unfair it may be, but I believe one of the rules of public service is that one's family – rightly or wrongly – is also put under the public spotlight.

From columns by Henry McNulty in *The Hartford* (Conn.) *Courant*. Reprinted with permission.

16-4. A hero's private life

    This exercise is based on the case of Oliver Sipple, the man who saved President Gerald Ford's life by deflecting Sara Jane Moore's arm and preventing her from shooting. Columnist Herb Caen of the *San Francisco Chronicle* revealed that Sipple was gay, but his family didn't know. Sipple sued the paper and lost. In the 1970s when this occurred, homosexuality was not accepted. Discuss what might happen today and if the climate is different. Is the ethical principle different now? Was this an invasion of privacy in an ethical sense, if not in a legal one?

16-5. Anonymous sources

    The issues here are similar to those in the textbook case. In this case, discuss whether the senator's bid for re-election makes a difference in reasons to publish. Discuss the public good vs. anonymous sources. During the Clinton/Lewinsky scandal, the media relied heavily on anonymous sources. Discuss whether students would have used anonymous sources to reveal some of the initial coverage in the presidential scandal.

16-6. Cooperating with police

Several newspapers have faced this dilemma, and during the 1990s this issue of cooperating with police caused heated debate. *The Hartford Courant* and other newspapers did print the names of "johns," citing public good. They said prostitution was a problem, and cooperating with the police was warranted in this case. For discussion: Would cooperation in this case lead to other cases where police would expect the newspaper to cooperate? What harm would printing the names of the men do? In some cases the men were prominent citizens. Years ago in a similar case, a man committed suicide. Does this type of exposure cause that risk? What would the newspaper do if someone did threaten to commit suicide if his name were printed? When police release so many names, how can you be sure they are accurate? What are the alternatives? Should you wait until these people are arraigned or convicted? Will you do follow-up stories if they are or are not convicted?

16-7. Personal dilemma

Students who have had internships often have personal experiences they want to relate. Would they make the same decision now, after using ethical guidelines, as they did at the time?

16-8. Code of ethics

I do this with my ethics class as a group activity. If time permits, I would do this with a basic reporting class. I ask students to devise a code of ethics for a campus publication, radio or TV station. Put the students in groups of three to five so they have to argue about their decisions. I suggest the following topics: Use of deception, accepting gifts or free tickets, anonymous sources, altering photographs, conflicts of interest – socializing with sources. The latter can provoke interesting discussion. Encourage students to access codes of ethics linked to the Web site for this book for guidance.

Multicultural Sensitivity 17

Goals

- To help students develop sensitivity to multicultural issues
- To teach students guidelines for reporting and writing about racial, ethnic and minority groups

Although this chapter is devoted to multicultural issues, the need to make students aware of sensitivity to these topics should be stressed throughout the course. I have attempted to do that by reminding students to gather multicultural sources in the chapters about sources and interviewing and when applicable elsewhere in the book. Because the issue is so important, however, I believe it is valuable to discuss it in a separate chapter and to devote at least one or more lessons to sensitivity training.

The concept of political correctness has become so controversial that your students may object to much information in this chapter or the entire book. If that is the case, their attitudes should generate excellent discussions. Many racial and ethnic media groups have Web sites offering excellent information and support. Encourage students to check these sites linked to the Web site for this book:
http://info.wadsworth.com/rich.

Teaching Suggestions

This chapter lends itself more to discussion and reporting activities than to writing exercises. Students should be cautioned that when they seek information about diversity, they need to be open-minded. They may try to prove a hypothesis that racial and ethnic groups are poorly treated by the media, and as a result, they may ignore positive comments. You can also discuss the fallacy of objectivity in connection with this chapter. Ask students to discuss how their own backgrounds preclude them from being totally objective.

One of the most successful exercises I used recently was a class project of the multicultural faces on campus. Each student wrote a brief vignette of a student from various countries, ethnic backgrounds or other types of diversity such as a blind student. We produced the package for the campus newspaper and I also created it online so all the students could get their brief profiles published. The vignettes turned out to be very interesting because the students who were interviewed had such diverse backgrounds and experiences, and the students in the class felt that they had learned something by interviewing people who differed considerably from them.

Here are a variety of suggestions not mentioned in the textbook or workbook. There are probably too many suggestions here to include in one lesson of a comprehensive reporting and writing course. Choose or adapt any of these that suit your needs

- Discuss the pros and cons of affirmative action. Invite a representative from your university's Office of Affirmative Action to class and have her or him discuss the topic and the university's efforts to improve diversity. (See next suggestion for preparation.)
- Invite a diversity trainer or the head of your campus diversity organization to class to do sensitivity training about multicultural issues.
- Ask students to gather statistics about minorities in the student body and in the faculty. Using the U.S. Census or the *Statistical Abstract* for your state (or for the United States), ask students to find out the percentage of minorities in the state and nationally, and compare the results to the percentage of minorities on campus. You could also ask them to do this for gender and compare the percentage of women on the faculty to women in the student body and in the national population
- Invite members or leaders of a campus or community minority group (preferably non-journalists) to class and discuss their perceptions of how the media portrays their groups. Include representatives of gay and lesbian groups and people with disabilities.
- Ask students to interview one or more minority journalists (either from ethnic, racial or social minority groups) or invite a journalist from a minority group to class. Discuss the journalist's personal experiences – if any – with prejudice in the newsroom or community, and the person's feelings about the impact minority journalists can make on the media. (Again, warn students to seek positive as well as negative responses.) Also reinforce the idea that one person's views do not represent an entire minority group.
- Interview some people over age 65 about their perceptions of media coverage for people in their age range. What kinds of stories do they prefer? What topics are they interested in reading about? Do they

116

favor a special section for older citizens? Do they think their interests and their generation are well represented in the media?

- Stories about people with disabilities: In an article in *Quill* magazine (May 1992), William G. Stothers said that although stories about people with disabilities are often lovingly told, the stories portray heroes and victims. He said an estimated 43 million Americans have a disability, but few stories represent the majority of those people – the workers, the professionals, the average people living average lives. "Welcome to the pity party, as it is called in the disability community," wrote Stothers, managing editor of *Mainstream,* the national magazine for people with disabilities. Using those comments as a springboard, ask to students to analyze the stories about people with disabilities and see if the sources are treated as heroes or victims. Do these stories portray people as extraordinary? Are they "gawking" stories, focused around the person's disability rather than other accomplishments?
- AIDS project: Several few years ago *The Philadelphia Inquirer* produced a project called "AIDS: A day with a global killer." It was a massive project in which 23 reporters and six photographers were sent to different places all over the world to write and photograph stories about how AIDS affected people – from relatives of people ho had died to care-givers. And they had to file their stories on the same day, on deadline, to represent one day in the life of AIDS. You can adapt the concept for a class project, asking each student to write a story about how AIDS affects different people in your community.
- AIDS awareness: Ask students to interview a random group (perhaps 10) of students about their perceptions of AIDS. Include questions such as how do you think AIDS is acquired, do you take precautions against the disease when you engage in sex, what is the difference between HIV and AIDS, and other questions that can be answered with facts. Then assign students to gather facts about AIDS and compare the perceptions of the people they interviewed with the facts to determine if students are truly informed about the disease.

Textbook Exercises

These exercises are self-explanatory. You can expand No. 4 to include an analysis of bylines; how many stories are written by women and men and whether there are differences in the types of stories male and female reporters cover.

I have had excellent results with No. 5, the multicultural vignette. Students said they were enlightened after doing the interviews. One African-American student leader who was interviewed complained that the questions were loaded, but after discussing his feelings with me, he lauded the exercise and volunteered to come to the class and speak. If you do not have students of varied racial and ethnic backgrounds in your class, you can ask students to invite their sources. If your class is multiculturally diverse, you could do the survey in the class and follow it by discussion.

A discussion of how students define race based on Meta Carstarphen's research can be fascinating. In her research, she found that journalists had many different definitions. My students also defined race in many different ways -- often based on culture rather than genetics. Discuss what these definitions mean to people's perceptions of race.

Workbook Exercises

17-1. Media survey

You can tailor this assignment to the needs of your class. If you have students who plan careers in public relations, ask them to interview officials of those organizations. This assignment can work effectively as a class project, with each student interviewing people from a different organization. Ask students to submit a memo about the organizations they plan to survey so you don't have several students interviewing the same people. Stress that this will be an unscientific survey, but it may provide insight for the students about the need for more minorities in the media.

If you prefer to extend this assignment, you can ask students to research national statistics. Every year *Press Woman* and *The American Editor*, the publication of the American Society of Newspaper Editors, publish annual surveys about the numbers of women and minorities in the newspaper industry, and other surveys about the broadcast industry are available in *Journalism Quarterly* or *Journalism Educator*. For discussion, include the concern over the term "qualified," a term that many media critics have criticized as a weak excuse by editors for not hiring minorities and as a racial slur.

17-2. Photo sensitivity

This assignment is intended to help students become sensitive to the fact that even though they may have good intentions and think they are portraying people in a positive light when selecting photographs, their actions can be offensive to members of minority groups. When students analyze the photographs in their local newspaper or others you assign, if you do not have students from various minority groups in class, invite members of those groups to class for the discussion. Ask students to make copies of the photographs they analyzed so you can distribute them to the class.

17-3. Gender stereotypes

Studies several years ago concluded that women were portrayed more in the kitchen and for hygiene products than men were. In the past 10 years, television commercials have changed considerably to reflect women in more professional roles, sometimes at the expense of men who are portrayed negatively. However, there are still many commercials that use women as sex objects, particularly the beer and some automobile advertisements. Discuss whether women and men in the class had different perceptions.

You could videotape some of these commercials for discussion in class, if you prefer. If your journalism program includes courses in advertising, ask the professors who teach the courses; they may have good materials to share with you for such discussions. Other good resources should be available in a women's studies department, if you have one at your university or college.

17-4. Age perceptions

This is an unscientific survey, and students should not put any credence in its findings. However, it can reveal interesting perceptions. I used this exercise in class several years ago and found that the few students I had in their 30s, 40s and 50s had very different perceptions from the majority of students in their early 20s. I was amazed that some students thought people in their 40s were "elderly," and I turned it into an article ("Never Call Them 'Spry,' " *Quill,* February 1989). The AP stylebook can be used as a guide for age (it says elderly and senior citizen should not be used for anyone under 65).

Reinforce the concept of avoiding adjectives and labeling people. Because so many journalists are in their 20s and 30s, articles about people in their 60s and older often contain ageist references. Discuss how journalists' perceptions creep into articles through clichés, assumptions (rocking chair images) and other inappropriate descriptions. Reinforce the dangers of adjectives and the need for reporters to beware of their own prejudices, perceptions and lack of objectivity.

Beat Reporting

18

This chapter will offer students a chance to brainstorm ideas for covering beats for print and online publications. Many beat reporting sources are available online. Check the Web site for this book for links to them: *http:info.wadsworth.com/rich.*

Teaching Suggestions

Many professors prefer to assign students to cover a science or environmental story, a business story and other specialty beats. If you have students who are interested in specializing in a particular area, you can ask them to cover that area as a beat throughout the semester. You might also try to have them cover beats that aren't covered by the campus newspaper and submit their stories for publication.

I have tried several approaches to teaching beat reporting. Recently I assigned students beats that were not covered by the campus newspaper and required them to turn in story budgets of three beat story ideas a week. In addition, I required them to write a news brief on their beat each week. We compiled the briefs from the class into a column of news briefs that we published in a weekly column in the campus newspaper. Periodically, I assigned the students to develop a full story from one of their briefs or news releases.

I now require students to check online resources for almost every story and especially if they are assigned to beats. The media resources for beat reporters are exceptional, and many are linked to the Web site for this chapter. Encourage students to use the Web for background, but also urge them to check posting dates of sites to make sure information is current and to evaluate the credibility of the sources.

Textbook Exercises

1. Business feature

Students should be able to find many business stories because most communities have businesses opening or closing, thriving or suffering. Alter this story to suit your needs. You might find a business story on campus as well. Discuss the economic aspects of a new program, a department or other business matters at your college or university. Students have difficulty asking specifics about how much a business earns, and sources are often reluctant to reveal this information. Students can ask for an estimated range or check if the company is publicly owned. Caution students to avoid flooding their stories with statistics and to explain any jargon.

2. Specialty subject

Encourage students to do background research using databases or library research before they interview their sources.

3. Interview a beat reporter

As an alternative to having students do individual stories, you could invite a reporter to class, particularly if many people in your class have a common interest, such as sports. Do a group interview and ask students to write a story. If students are interviewing different reporters, check first to make sure several students don't interview the same reporter. If they do choose the same person, you could have them do this as a group interview.

4. Internet sources

If you have done the scavenger hunts in Chapter 6, Sources and Online Research, your students should be somewhat familiar with the wealth of Internet sources. Now have them tailor it to their beats. Many directories for beat resources are linked to this chapter's Web site or refer students back to Chapter 6.

5. List beats

You can assign students to specific beats or let them choose ones they prefer. You might also ask students to devise story ideas for beats they would like to cover.

Workbook Exercises

18-1. Beat story ideas

Students can do this assignment without actually contacting people, so you can avoid having too many students on campus bothering the same sources. After you have discussed their beat preferences, you can assign beats to make sure students are not contacting the same people. You could invite editors from your campus newspaper to class to discuss which beats or areas of the campus don't get much coverage. For example, even though a campus reporter might cover housing, various residence halls or scholarship halls may not get much attention. Within the campus administration, there may also be many departments that don't receive much coverage. The same situation may exist in your community if you have a small local newspaper.

18-2. Briefs or press releases

As mentioned in the teaching suggestions, I ask students to write at least a brief each week pertaining to their beat, and we use these in the campus newspaper. The news brief or press release is not as demanding as a full story, which is often too strenuous for as a weekly assignment for a beginning reporting class. However, the briefs can be precursors to larger stories.

18-3. Analyze beat coverage

You can do this in a class period if you prefer or assign it for homework. To encourage discussion, you might consider pairing students or putting them in groups and having them analyze several days or a week's worth of campus and/or local newspapers. Ask them to discuss how they are affected by the stories that are covered and what kinds of stories would make them more interested in the beat.

18-4. Analyze a beat story

Ask students to write a list of questions that would improve a published story or ask them to list questions to expand a brief from one of their beats. How much more information would they need to make it a full story?

18-5. Team beats

Several newspapers have tried team beat coverage to replace traditional beats. Teams of reporters and editors are assigned to topics, such as shopping, lifestyles, culture as well as the traditional beats of government, crime and education. Discuss what traditional beats, such as city hall, education, state government, and so on do students think should be covered as they were in the past? What kinds of beats do they expect to cover in newspapers of the future? For story planning, students often work well in groups. Either assign or let them choose team beats.

18-6. Online newspaper beats

You might ask students to check various online college or commercial newspapers to get ideas for interactive features. Ask them to consider what kinds of questions, features, quizzes or columns they or their friends would respond to in an on-line newspaper.

Discuss the lack of space restrictions that online newspapers have, resulting in the possibility of maintaining huge amounts of copy. For example, they can keep the original documents of any agency online, including the university budget, complete statistics of all athletic contests, and volumes of general information. What kinds of information would they find most useful to have at their disposal? You might brainstorm this topic in connection with a back-to-school edition. What kinds of information would new or returning students find most helpful?

18-7. Analysis of beat resources

This exercise is intended to familiarize students with the wealth of beat resources available to them and to get them started in checking the Internet regularly for resources. The answers to these questions can vary. Encourage students to feel free to criticize these sites and analyze their resources and ease of use.

Obituaries

19

Goals

- To teach students form for basic obituaries
- To teach students how to write feature obituaries
- To teach students to search the Internet for obituary information
- To teach the following style concepts: Abbreviation of states (AP style instead of postal service), no apostrophe for plural of years, time (a.m., p.m.) wording of specific masses, recognizing euphemisms for death, titles for clergy, master's degree, numbers, addresses.

Teaching Suggestions

This chapter is one of the easiest for students to master because the form for obituaries is so specific. In fact, some of my colleagues teach obituaries on the first day of the semester to give students a sense of accomplishment. However, I prefer to wait until they have mastered other basic skills, because I don't want students to think all news writing is so formulated. Also, the feature obituaries require more skills, and students can get the mistaken idea that obituaries take little effort. The obituary form is easy to teach, but you need to stress the style for various church services.

A common teaching technique is to have students write their own obituaries, but I urge you to avoid this. Although students seem to enjoy making up the cause of their own demise, many students are facing serious or life-threatening diseases, such as cancer, AIDS, and others. In one semester alone, two of my female students had uterine cancer, another was facing gall bladder surgery and another had throat cancer. Another semester one of my students had the HIV-virus. In addition, many students have experienced the death of friends and family members, so I think it is too insensitive to write personal obituaries.

Textbook Exercises

1. Celebrity obituary

This activity can reinforce some of the research skills in Chapter 6. Students can use Obits.com online at *www.obituary.com,* other online sources or printed sources such as *Contemporary Authors,* encyclopedias, almanacs and newspapers and magazines to research an obituary about a celebrity. To give them additional practice writing basic obituaries, you could ask students to write their celebrity obituary in abbreviated basic form and also in feature form. Several of the workbook exercises will provide more practice in basic form.

2. Jim Henson obituary

This obituary was selected because most students can relate to Henson and the Muppets. The quotes are limited in this, so the basic obituary form can apply. A sample appears in the discussion section. Here is a version of the Jim Henson obituary.

Jim Henson, creator of the Muppets that delighted millions of children who watched Sesame Street, died yesterday [use the day of the week]. He was 53.

Henson died at a New York hospital 20 hours after entering with a bacterial infection, streptococcus pneumonia.

Considered one of the most famous puppeteers in the World, Mr. Henson created Kermit the Frog, Miss Piggy, Big Bird and the Cookie Monster. His puppets, a combination of hand puppets and marionettes appeared on the public television show, "Sesame Street," which is seen in more than 80 countries.

Mr. Henson was born in Greenville, Miss., and grew up in Washington, D.C. He began his career as a puppeteer when he was a theater major at the University of Maryland. When he was a freshman in college, he had his first television show, "Sam and Friends."

In 1956 he built a hand puppet called Kermit, one of his most famous Muppets. "I suppose that he's an alter ego," Mr. Henson once said. "But he's a little snarkier than I am – slightly wise. Kermit says things I hold myself back from saying."

In the 1960s he began appearing with his puppets on "The Ed Sullivan Show," and nine years later, when the creators of Children's Television Workshop began "Sesame Street," Mr. Henson's puppets were featured.

"Jim was dedicated to children's education, and with all his commercial success, he never lost his idealism," said Joan Ganz Cooney, chief executive of Children's Television Workshop.

Peggy Charren, founder of Action for Children's Television, said, "He could make you laugh while you were crying."

In 1976, Mr. Henson gained fame with his own show, "The Muppet Show," which featured Kermit and Miss Piggy and was seen in more than 100 countries by an estimated 235 million viewers.

When he died, Mr. Henson was in the midst of concluding a deal with the Walt Disney Co. to acquire Henson Associates, Inc., which owns the Muppets, for a price estimated at $100 million to $150 million.

Erwin Okum, spokesman for Walt Disney Co., said, "I never met a kinder, gentler, wonderful soul in the entertainment industry or anywhere."

Mr. Henson lived in Manhattan, but he also had homes in California, Connecticut and London.

He is survived by his wife, the former Jane Nebel, and five children.

The family is planning a memorial service but details have not been announced.

Officials from the Public Broadcasting Company said in a prepared statement: "His legacy is the lesson that one can both laugh and learn."

Portions taken from *The New York Times*. Used with permission.

Workbook Exercises

19-1. Basic obituaries

Each of the obituaries in the workbook is designed to provide practice in dealing with style.

a. Burnside obituary: This exercise emphasizes the most basic obituary form. The death notice includes words that should be omitted from the obituary, such as "beloved" and "devoted" and the euphemism, "passed away."

Samuel Morris Burnside, a retired real estate broker who lived in Southwest Portland, died of heart failure Monday in the Portland Care Center. He was [calculate the age when you write this].

He was born in Weber Utah, and was reared on a farm near Grant, Idaho. He attended the University of Idaho and Albin Normal School. Mr. Burnside moved to the Portland area from Jerome, Idaho in 1942.

He worked as a real estate broker in the Southwest Portland area for many years until his retirement. Mr. Burnside was a past president and lieutenant governor of Division 64 of the Kiwanis Pacific Northwest District.

Survivors include his sons, Harold G. of Salem and Dr. Robert M. of Springfield, 10 grandchildren, eight great-grandchildren; and two great-great grandchildren.

A funeral will be at 1 p.m. Friday in the chapel of Young's Funeral Home in Tigard. Burial will be in Crescent Grove Cemetery.

The family suggests that remembrances be contributions to the Southwest Hills Kiwanis Club.

Based on an obituary from *The Oregonian*. Reprinted with permission.

b. Sullivan obituary: This obituary should use the courtesy title, "Ms." and proper style for states, not postal service abbreviations. Some newspapers include visitation and a parent or child who died before the subject of the obituary, but other newspapers do not. Students should avoid euphemisms for death.

Services for Sandra K. Sullivan, director of the Foundation for Independent Living, will be at 10 a.m. Saturday in St. Paul's Baptist Church, 9030 Addison Place [your town]. Visitation is from 9 a.m. to 9 p.m. Friday at the church. Burial is private.

Ms. Sullivan died in her home of cancer Saturday. She was -- [calculate her age based on her birth date when you write this].

A lifelong resident [of your town], Ms. Sullivan had worked for 20 years with the foundation, the last 10 as its director.

She was an accomplished pianist and choir musical director for St. Paul's Baptist Church.

Ms. Sullivan was born in [your town] and graduated from (your town) High School. She received her bachelor's degree in social work from Michigan State University and a master's degree in social work from New York University.

She is survived by her mother, Zoe Margolis of [your town];sons, Christopher and Vernon of (your town), and son, Archie of Lansing, Mich.; a daughter, Mattie Hills of San Francisco, Calif.

The family requests that remembrances be made to the Sandra K. Sullivan musical scholarships at the church.

c. Huff obituary: This exercise is about a man who had AIDS. Although it is rarely included now, the probability exists that same-sex partners in long-term relationships or marriages will be listed as survivors in more obits in the future. Jim Nicholson includes partners as survivors in his obituaries in the *Philadelphia Daily News*. The exercise also teaches students to avoid euphemisms, such as "entered into rest." The obituary also tests relatives to exclude, such as the name of the aunt. For style, students should capitalize Mass of Christian Burial.

Brett Stephen Huff, a graphic designer, died Monday at his parents' home [in your town] of illness related to AIDS. He was -- [whatever age you calculate from 1965].

Mr. Huff was diagnosed with AIDS in 1994 while he was living in Los Angeles, where he worked for the Tucker Design Group. He returned in 1995 to be near his family, and he started his own firm, Huff Designs.

In the past year he spoke to students in area high schools to educate them about AIDS.

"He wanted to alert people to ways of preventing AIDS," said his mother, Martha Huff. "He tried to make people

more sensitive to people who have the disease."

A native of [your town], Mr. Huff graduated from [your town] High School and earned a bachelor's degree in art from the University of Missouri in Columbia, Mo.

A Mass of Christian Burial will be celebrated at 10:30 a.m. (use tomorrow's day) at Our Savior Church, 2020 Marysville Ave. Burial will be in Greenlawn Cemetery,30 Main St., [your town].

Contributions may be made to the AIDS Research Fund, Fernwood Hospital, 373 Paloma Street, [your town].

This obituary of Jerry Garcia does not exactly follow the information in the workbook, but it can be distributed as an example of how to combine factual and reaction information in a feature obituary. The workbook exercise contains more information from other sources. This exercise can be used as is or you can ask students to do more research on the Internet. As explained in the workbook, there are several sources of information about Jerry Garcia and the Grateful Dead on the World Wide Web, and it would be a good exercise for students to see what they can find from Internet sources. The easiest way to access Internet sites about Garcia is to use a search engine such as google.com.

This obituary can generate some good discussion about whether to include negative factors, such as the drug addiction, of the deceased in an obit. Most students will mention Garcia's addiction, but are more reluctant to include a criminal record of a person who died. Discuss when such information is relevant and should be included. In this case, the drug problem is definitely relevant, particularly because Garcia died in a drug treatment center.

Jerry Garcia

SAN FRANCISCO (AP) - Jerry Garcia, the master guitarist whose band the Grateful Dead symbolized the 1960s counterculture and remained a top concert draw three decades later, died today at a drug treatment center. He was 53.

The cause was a heart attack, the Marin County sheriff's office said.

He was found in his bed at 4:23 a.m. by a counselor at Serenity Knolls, a residential treatment center for drug addiction in Forest Knolls. Garcia had a long history of drug abuse.

A nurse attempted CPR, and sheriff's department staff who were summoned also failed to revive him, said Dan Murphy, a sheriff's spokesman.

Word of Garcia's death quickly spread, especially on the Internet, where the Grateful Dead has an exceptionally wide following.

Within an hour, the Sausalito-based Well computer network posted a notice that it was clogged by fans sharing their grief:

"The WELL is currently experiencing a system slowdown. There is an influx to discuss the passing of the Grateful Dead's Jerry Garcia."

The Grateful Dead, with its roots in the Bay Area's psychedelic scene of the 1960s, combined rock, bluegrass, blues and folk influences into a unique stew. Garcia was lead guitarist, composer and sometime vocalist.

Among the band's best known songs were "Truckin'," "Casey Jones," and "Friend of the Devil." Its only top 10 hit was the 1987 song "Touch of Grey," with its refrain "I will survive."

But the Dead was almost more a way of life than a band to the thousands of "Deadheads," many of whom followed the group from concert to concert.

They made the band one of the most popular concert draws in the United States, grossing tens of millions of dollars each year.

"You need music," Garcia once said. "I don't know why; it's probably one of those Joe Campbell questions, why we need ritual. We need magic, and bliss, and power, myth, and celebration and religion in our lives, and music is a good way to encapsulate a lot of it."

In concert, Garcia was either spotty or spectacular. In the 1980s and 1990s, he would forget lyrics or strain to hit high notes when he sang slow-tempo standards such as "Sugaree," "Althea" and "Ship of Fools."

But his searing, improvised guitar solos breathed new life into even the band's most overworked numbers, sending dancing Deadheads into paroxysms of glee through the extended jams.

He rarely spoke on stage, reportedly because he feared how his words would be interpreted by rabid fans who analyzed every nuance.

The bearded, rotund Garcia had a history of health problems that occasionally caused breaks in the Dead's grueling concert schedule. In 1986, he entered the hospital in a diabetic coma.

Garcia slimmed down, stopped smoking, cut down on drugs and hired a personal fitness trainer after falling ill with exhaustion in 1991. But the years of constant touring took its toll.

"It was a meltdown. Too many cigarettes, too much junk food and too little exercise," band spokesman Dennis McNally said last year.

McNally said he didn't know why Garcia was at the treatment center.

"It was news to me," he said. "I thought he was going to Hawaii. Apparently he was paying increased attention to his health." He said he had seen Garcia recently, so he could not have been in the center for more than a couple of days.

Garcia was born Aug. 1, 1942, in San Francisco. His Spanish-born father was a musician, playing reed instruments and leading a swing band; his grandmother, who largely raised him, founded a union for laundry workers.

He became interested in electric guitar and painting as a teen-ager, taking classes at what is now the San Francisco Art Institute. He also spent hours in the coffee bars of North Beach, reading Beat writers like Jack Kerouac and soaking up the beatnik atmosphere.

After a brief stint in the Army, Garcia formed several folk and bluegrass bands. In 1964, he founded a band called the Warlocks, which also included Bob Weir, Bill Kreutzmann, Ron "Pigpen" McKernan and Phil Lesh. But there was already a band by that name. They found another name in the dictionary.

"We never decided to be the Grateful Dead," he told Rolling Stone. "What happened was the Grateful Dead came up as a suggestion because we were at Phil's house one day; he had a big Oxford dictionary, I opened it up and the first thing I saw was The Grateful Dead.

"It said that on the page and it was so astonishing. It was truly weird, a truly weird moment."

A grateful dead is a type of traditional British folk ballad in which a human helps a ghost of someone who has died recently find peace. "They're about karma, which is apt," said McNally.

The band itself lost several members over its many years. McKernan died in 1973 of the affects of alcoholism. Keyboardist Keith Godchaux died in 1980 in a car crash a year after he left the band. Another keyboardist, Brent Mydland, died in 1990 of a drug overdose.

Garcia is survived by his third wife, Deborah Koons Garcia, a Marin County filmmaker, and four daughters; Heather, 32, Annabelle, 25, Teresa, 21 and Keelin, 6. Funeral arrangements were not immediately announced.

Elizabeth Weise, The Associated Press. Printed with permission.

19-3. Online obituary

This exercise will help students visualize how to organize material for a Web obituary. You can ask them to write a standard obituary in print form. They should also search for related links. If you wish to use a politician or celebrity in your area, you could suggest that students create a timeline of highlights of the person's career. This also will give the students a chance to do online research.

19-4. Style quiz corrections

Corrections are in boldface type.

1. He is survived by his sons in Lansing, MI. **(Mich.)** and a daughter in Dallas, TX. **(Texas. – Dallas does not require a state, but if it is used, it should not be abbreviated.)**

2. Jim Henson began appearing on television with the Muppets in the 1960's **(1960s.)**

3. Funeral **(omit funeral - optional)** services will be held **(eliminate held)** at 1 P.M. **(p.m.)** Friday.

4. A mass of Christian burial **(Mass of Christian Burial)** will be held **celebrated)** at 10:30 a.m. Thursday.

5. She passed away **(died)** on September 9, **(Sept. 9,)** 1992.

6. Father **(The Rev.)** James Flanagan is the priest at the roman catholic church **(Roman Catholic Church)** in our town.

7. She received her masters **(master's)** degree from Florida State University.

8. Survivors include fifteen **(15)** grandchildren and six great grandchildren **(great-grandchildren).**

9. Interment **(Burial is preferred)** will be in the Greenlawn Cemetary **(Cemetery).**

10. She lived at 1,200 Westside Rd. **(1200 Westside Road).**

Speeches, News Conferences and Meetings

20

Goals

- To teach students how to select quotes for speeches
- To teach students how to cover news conferences and meetings
- To encourage critical thinking
- To familiarize students with online speeches and press conference resources
- Style concepts: Titles, vote count, constitutional, First Amendment, spelling, money, no apostrophe with plural for years.

Teaching Suggestions

This chapter will reinforce the importance of taking good notes to get full quotes for speeches and press conferences. It also aims to help students become selective about quotes, especially when writing speech and meeting stories.

The best way to teach students how to write speech stories is to have them attend speeches and meetings on campus or in the community. If you use the speeches in this chapter, read them aloud and let students write from their notes. Then ask them to check their quotes for accuracy by reading the written text in their workbooks or distribute the speech. If possible, obtain videotapes of speeches, press conferences and meetings and use them in place of these exercises so students get practice taking notes from spoken material.

Another source of speeches is the Internet. You can find many speeches about journalism linked to the Web site for this book. If you have audio capabilities in your computer laboratory, you could have students listen to speeches. Many of the historical speeches are available in audio form or access whitehouse.com for White House press conferences online in print or audio form. The Vonnegut speech is a fun exercise and also should alert students to be careful about trusting everything they read online.

Coaching To help students learn selectivity for quotes, especially in speech and press conference stories, ask them to go through their notes and identify quotes that might serve as pull quotes to be highlighted with the stories. These can be a guide for choosing the quotes that should be included in the stories. For meeting stories, ask students to write a highlights or facts box. That will serve as an organizational device and help them determine the most important information to include in their stories.

Textbook Exercises

1. Burl Osborne speech

This speech can be read aloud to give students practice taking notes or you can have students download the text from the book's Web site for exercises for this chapter. The speech takes about 20 minutes to read. Ask students to put a pull quote at the top of their story. After students have written their stories (before or after you have edited them), you might ask them to check their quotes in the textbook version. I ask students to write at the bottom of their papers the quotes or information they wish they had included but didn't because of poor judgment or poor note taking. This speech can take a hard or soft lead. Remind students not to flood the lead with details of where and when. Here are some examples of students' leads:

Pull quote: "Censorship on the campus today will be censorship in the newsroom tomorrow."

Hard-news lead: Burl Osborne, editor of *The Dallas Morning News,* warned journalism students yesterday about the dangers of restricting free speech.

Osborne gave the speech to about 100 students at Stauffer-Flint Hall. A growing number of campuses now forbid offensive speech or expression, he said.

"These concerns are especially important to journalists because censorship on the campus today will be censorship in the newsroom tomorrow."

Anecdotal lead: At the University of Connecticut, inappropriate laughter and excluding people from conversations is against school speech codes. At the University of Minnesota, a male professor was charged with sexual harassment for failing to greet a female student. At Smith College students were given a list of terms of oppression, which included the word "lookism," bias based on attractiveness.

"I predict that the next ism might be heightism, whose victims may not be considered short but vertically challenged," said Burl Osborne, *Dallas Morning News* editor and president of the American Society of Newspaper Editors.

Osborne spoke to journalism students yesterday in Stauffer-Flint Hall.

2. Online speeches

The link to the Kurt Vonnegut spoof graduation speech is fun for students. You can download this without telling them and read it in class. Other online speech stories abound, many in audio form so students can gain practice taking notes.

3. News Conference: Richard Jewell remarks

I have selected this press conference because the comments Richard Jewell made included very emotional quotes. The object is to help students recognize how to use emotional quotes high in a speech, although I don't like them to start speeches with quotes. The Richard Jewell case also posed great ethical dilemmas for the media. Jewell is now a police officer in Georgia, but he recently said he will never get rid of the stigma the media coverage caused. Check the Web site for this chapter for links to CNN's Olympic Park bombing coverage if you want to assign students more background. Here is the AP story about the press conference:

ATLANTA -- For 88 days, Richard Jewell stoically stood his ground, professing his innocence while he was branded the FBI's chief suspect in the Olympic park pipe bombing. Finally cleared by prosecutors, the weight of suspicion lifted, he let down his guard and cried.

The tears came Monday as he recalled the bodies of friends injured by the blast, and when he turned to his mother, who buried her head in her hand.

"Mom, thanks for standing by me and believing in me," he said, his voice choking. "I love you."

Another emotion -- anger -- came out as he lashed out at reporters and investigators who had depicted him as the man who brought the specter of terrorism to the Summer Olympics. But at the end of the press conference, he calmly delivered a message.

"I thank God that it has now ended, and that you now know what I have known all along," he said in a firm voice. "I am an innocent man." The July 27 bomb blast at Centennial Olympic Park -- the informal gathering place for spectators at the Games -- killed one woman outright, was blamed for a cameraman's death and injured more than 100.

Jewell initially was hailed as a hero for alerting authorities to suspicious knapsack and helping to evacuate the area. He gave numerous interviews until, three days after the bombing, The Atlanta Journal-Constitution reported he was a suspect. Reporters staked out his apartment complex for days and followed his every move, while Jewell refused to comment. His mother, Barbara, in August

tearfully begged President Clinton to "end this nightmare."

"I felt like a hunted animal, followed constantly, waiting to be killed," Jewell said. "The media said I fit the profile of a lone bomber. That was a lie. The media said I was a frustrated police wanna-be. That was a lie. I was, then and now, a law enforcement officer."

On Saturday, federal prosecutors gave Jewell's attorneys a letter clearing him as a suspect. To Jewell and his attorneys, the letter is a weak attempt at an apology.

"While the government can tell you that I am an innocent man, the government's letter cannot give me back my good name or my reputation," Jewell said.

"In their mad rush to fulfill their own personal agendas, the FBI and the media almost destroyed me and my mother."

His lawyers plan to sue the Journal-Constitution and NBC for comments Tom Brokaw made in early news reports about the bombing. The Journal-Constitution on Monday defended its stories about Jewell as "accurate and appropriate."

A lawsuit against the FBI is being considered.

"I don't have enough words, I can't cuss enough, to describe the way they have treated this man," said Watson Bryant, one of Jewell's lawyers.

He also lashed out at the FBI over affidavits released Monday that were used to gain warrants for searches of Jewell's home and other property in the days after the bombing, saying they are "full of half-truths."

The papers, which a judge had ordered unsealed with names blacked out, quote several acquaintances speaking of Jewell's fascination with police work. They also quote witnesses who saw Jewell in the vicinity of the explosion, but none who saw him handle the bomb.

"I think the American public should be shocked at how little it takes for the government to get a search warrant," Bryant said. "Who are these people?

"FBI spokesman Jay Spadafore declined to respond. As he did after the bombing, Jewell again Monday tried to place the hero label on others, such as officers who placed their bodies between the package and the crowd.

"When the explosion occurred, I saw my fellow officers and friends flying through the air. I saw people lying on the ground hurt, badly hurt," he said in a trembling voice. "I moved people away from the unattended package and I evacuated people from the sound tower. All I did was my job."

What Jewell now wants is a chance to restore his image and to try to pursue a career in the work that he loves.

"Anybody who knew me knows I could not hurt another person," he said. "I love people. I love children. I am a public servant. ... I don't look at law enforcement as a job."

4. Online news conferences

You can always check *www.whitehouse.gov* for online news conferences from the president's press secretary. The U.S. Census bureau, linked to this chapter's Web site, also has Webcasts of news releases as well as print transcripts. As always, it is preferable to have students cover an actual local government meeting, especially if you can accompany them. In my community, city commission meetings are televised, and I videotape one and use it in class so I can explain unfamiliar terms to students as thy watch it.

Workbook Exercises

20-1. Graduation Speech

This speech reinforces the fact that the best information is often toward the end of the speech. The emphasis in this story should be on Roger Fidler's comments about the future of journalism and job opportunities for graduates in a world of changing technology. Students should build their lead from the last part of the speech when Fidler gives his predictions. Information about Fidler's background should be in the middle or lower in the story. The second or third paragraph should explain where and when he gave the speech.

Although this is a rather typical graduation speech, it does not contain many good quotes. Stress that students should paraphrase and summarize information instead of using dull quotes.

Here is a student's story of Fidler's speech:

Roger Fidler used Bob Dylan's song, "The Times Are A Changin'," as the focus of his commencement speech yesterday at the University of Kansas.

"For those who can adapt to change, the future is bright," said Fidler, a professor at the Kent State University and former director of new media for Knight-Ridder Inc.

Speaking before an audience of 2,000 people in Memorial stadium, Fidler said he did not want to fool the graduates by painting a rosy picture of the future. He said they were entering a world of change.

He said that job changes and new technology will replace job longevity. He cited his own first-hand experience.

In his 20-year career, Fidler changed jobs nine times. He began his career as a science writer for the Eugene Register Guard.

"In most cases I created my own job and defined the position," he said. "This is the future that I believe awaits you."

Fidler, who developed the portable flat-panel computer, said that pigmented ink and pulp paper will give way to digital ink and portable information devices. The flat-panel computer, about the size of an 8- by 10-inch paper tablet, is intended as a device on which people may read their newspapers digitally in the future.

Even with the new technology, he said, the assumption that traditional media will be killed is a gross mistake. He said that the media characteristics that would be most valued in the future are credibility and connections to the community.

However, Fidler said the new technology would transform the world.

"When media historians a century from now look back on this decade and the first decade of the new millennium, the inventions of this period will be declared at least as significant . . . as the inventions of printing presses and movable type in the last half of the 15th century," he said.

Fidler said the future is bright for those who can accept change and continue growing.

"You will be the ones who actually transform media and shape the future," Fidler said. "May you all find the joy that comes from doing a job well."

20-2. Vonnegut hoax graduation speech - online

This should be a fun exercise for students. You can print out the speech and read it to students. Treat it as though it were an actual graduation speech. Students should stress the concepts of flossing, singing and other unusual factors in the lead. The nut graph should include when and where Kurt Vonnegut supposedly gave the speech. Follow with paraphrased comments interspersed with some wonderful quotes. Discuss the real hoax with students, and urge them to be careful before they pass information along via e-mail or trust information they receive without checking the source.

20-3. News conference

Here is how the Associated Press covered Michael Jordan's retirement news conference:

Jordan makes retirement official

By Rick Gano
AP Sports Writer

CHICAGO, Jan. 13 (AP) — The NBA's greatest player made it official today.

Michael Jordon retired from the Chicago Bulls after 13 seasons, six championships and countless soaring dunks. But he left open the possibility that he might return one day.

"Mentally, I'm exhausted. I don't feel I have a challenge," Jordan said at a news conference at the United Center, where a bronze statue of him stands outside. "Physically, I feel great.

"This is a perfect time for me to walk away from the game. I'm at peace with that."

Jordan said he was "99.9 percent" sure he would never return and added, "You can read that for what it's worth. . . .I'm very secure in my decision."

When pressed why he wouldn't say he was 100 percent certain, Jordan said: "Because it's my 1 percent and not yours."

Word of Jordan's retirement broke late Monday, but he had refused to comment until today. After leading the Bulls to their sixth championship in June, Jordan said he would make an announcement on his future only once the NBA lockout ended.

The players and owners reached a deal last week to save what's left of the season, and everyone's next question was whether Jordan would return.

The Jordan era included five MVP awards, 10 scoring titles, 12 All-Star appearances and many magic moments, from last-second shots to phenomenal scoring outbursts. More important, Jordan had charm and a nice-guy image that earned him multimillion-dollar sponsorship deals and reached even non-sport fans.

"I tried to be the best basketball player I could be," said Jordan, who was joined by his wife, Juanita, Bulls chairman Jerry Reinsdorf and NBA commissioner David Stern. "I've had a great time."

Jordan alluded to his first retirment in 1993, when he briefly pursued a professional baseball career before returning late in the 1994-95 season.

"Well, we do this again, a second time," he said to open the news conference.

At one point, the Bulls unveiled a banner in the rafters from Jordan's first retirement. It said, "Jordan 1984-1993" — but it will now have to be updated.

Asked if he had lost his desire to play, he said: "The desire is always going to be there." But he said he wanted to make sure that the desire was there "not one-fourth of the time I step onto the court, but every time."

Jordan, who had a bandage on his right index finger, said he severed a tendon while trying to cut a cigar and would need surgery. But he said he had already decided to retire before the accident.

"I'm just going to enjoy life and do things I've never done before," he said.

He said he looked forward to being a parent and would "live vicariously through my kids," whether or not they played basketball.

"My life will take a change," said Jordan, adding that he also will tend to his many business interests. He makes an estimated $45 million a year from endorsements.

Added his wife: "I see Michael doing a lot more carpooling."

Reinsdorf called Jordan's announcement "a tough day for basketball fans all over the world."

"This is a day I hoped would never come," he said.

Countered Stern: "I disagree with Jerry. This is a great day. The greatest basketball player in the history of the game is getting the opportunity to retire with the grace that described his play."

Jordan, 35, said he hoped the Bulls would re-sign teammate Scottie Pippen but added that was only his opinion and that he didn't know what decisions the team would make. Jordan met with a few teammates at his home Monday and told them the thought of playing an abbreviated, 50-game season wasn't enough of a challenge.

Now, Jordan goes out as he always wanted - on top. His last-second shot - the last one he ever took - gave the Bulls a victory over the Utah Jazz and their sixth title.

"There's a way to go out as an athlete, and that's the way to go out," said B.J. Armstrong, one of about a dozen players working out Tuesday at the Berto Center.

Armstrong, who now plays with Charlotte, is a good friend of Jordan's and a teammate on Chicago's first three NBA championship teams.

"He went out on top, he made the last shot, he made all the right plays. He's had a fabulous career and everything you could ever ask as an athlete, he's done. He had a chance to leave and this was the chance," Armstrong said.

Let students read the agenda and decide which item is worthy of an advance. Then ask them to write it based on the information in their workbooks. Here is how the local newspaper reporter covered the story:

City considers nudity ordinance

Lawrence city commissioners today said they favored adopting a proposed ordinance that would outlaw nudity in bars in the city.

The proposed ordinance would limit nudity in businesses licensed to serve alcohol.

"I'm not into banning free speech, or banning anything, but I am into putting some controls on entertainment that is not a benefit to the community," Commissioner Shirley Martin-Smith said. "People are just amazed that this even needs to be an issue."

Commissioners will discuss the proposal at their weekly meeting, beginning at 6:30 p.m. Monday in the City Commission meeting room at City Hall, Sixth and Massachusetts streets.

The proposed ordinance says that alcohol-licensed establishments that offer nude dancing "foster and promote incidents of criminal activity, can and do adversely affect property values, can and do contribute to neighborhood decay and blight, and do create direct exposures to health risks and potential health hazards."

The proposed city law would affect only businesses licensed to sell alcohol, and not other means of "adult entertainment," such as X-rated movies.

City Manager Mike Wildgen said the issue developed from a Johnson County man's recent request for information from the city about its nudity ordinances. The man was interested in opening a topless bar, so the city staff drafted an ordinance that would ban such nudity.

Martin-Smith favors it.

"I think the point of the ordinance is to eliminate the possibility of nudity as entertainment in the city," she said. "I think we just have to pursue it and see where it takes us, which is what we do on a lot of issues."

Commissioner Bob Schumm also favors a ban on public nudity.

"We just don't need it," he said. "We're doing fine without it. This is a wholesome city, a good place to raise a family and we don't need all the problems that go along with it (adult entertainment)."

Commissioner Bob Walters, who described himself as "not a prude," said that nude entertainment in any form simply should not be allowed in any business with access to the public.

"Sometimes I don't understand why we can't do what we think is in the best interests of the community," Walters said.

Johnson County currently is being sued by a club and several individual dancers who say that the county's ban on nude dancing is unconstitutional.

LeeAnne Gillaspie, the county's chief deputy counselor, said the legal basis for restricting behavior in such clubs was firmly stated in the 21st Amendment to the Constitution, which outlawed Prohibition and gave states power to restrict alcohol consumption. She said once the law moves away from alcohol, however, the issue moves into the First Amendment and freedom of expression guarantees.

Mark Fagan, *Lawrence* (Kan.) *Daily Journal-World*. Reprinted with permission.

This story lends itself to a creative lead because of the subject matter. The information about other matters was not part of this story but was added to the exercise notes because most meeting stories often include this type of material. You can ask students to write a one-issue story or add the other information at the end. Some of my students were very critical about the fact that the pig issue was more important than the loss of jobs in the police department, a good point for discussion. However, we discussed the fact that the pig issue dominated the meeting, it was highly emotional and the police budget cuts were approved without much comment. In a small local newspaper, the police cuts might have been a separate story, as well.

Here is the original:

Please make us pets, pig please

ST. PETERSBURG – Bo knows City Council.

Bo Jackswine, that is.

The 42-pound Vietnamese potbellied pig – named in honor of the athletic standout Bo Jackson – charmed council members Thursday into reconsidering a city-wide swine ban.

After seeing the pig in council chambers, council members voted unanimously to ask the city attorney to rework city laws to reclassify Vietnamese potbellied pigs as domestic animals. That would make it legal to keep them within city limits. Once the attorney revises the city law, it will go before council for another vote.

Bo's owner, Janie Finck, wore pig emblem earrings when she appeared before the council to extol the virtues of pig ownership. Finck was ecstatic when council members voted to look at making Bo a legal city resident. She had said she would move out of the city if the ban remained.

"Thank you very much," she said. "Bo thanks you very much. I am very happy. And Bo did excellent. He was definitely a ham."

Last week a majority of council members rejected an effort to modify a city law that prohibits swine within city limits. But after hearing from Finck, council member Edward L. Cole Jr. asked the council to reconsider. Finck decided to bring Bo to City Hall so council members could see a miniature pig for themselves.

The pig was a celebrity at City Hall. Adorned with a red bow around his neck, he swished his tail incessantly and walked to the end of his leash to sniff people curiously.

The pig's appearance was fodder for a string of jokes as council members expressed their support for modifying the pig ban.

"Let me mention that Bo Jackswine has been a constituent of mine for over year and there have been no complaints," said council member Robert Stewart. "He's a perfect neighbor."

Vice Mayor Charles Shorter was so impressed by the pig, he said he might consider getting one himself.

Mayor David Fischer added: "Talk about rolling over!"

After a time, Fischer put a halt to the pig puns.

"All right, let's have a swine call," Fischer said.

The vote to reconsider the swine ban was a relief to the half dozen pig owners who showed up at the 8 a.m. council meeting to show their support.

"I took off work," said Kris Guidice, who owns Popeye and Ryne, two Vietnamese potbellied pigs. "I haven't slept in two days because I've been so worried about it."

John Hood, who lives in St. Petersburg and owns Gidget, a white Vietnamese potbellied pig, said his pig means the world to him.

"It was either they pass it or I'd have moved out," Hood said. "You can steal my truck or anything else, but you better leave my pig alone."

In other business, the council unanimously agreed to cut five positions from the police department, despite strenuous objections from Police Chief Samuel Safety. He said the personnel cuts would hamper his department's ability to patrol the streets at a time when the crime rate is increasing.

Shorter said the police department could cut positions from its administrative and clerical staff. The cuts are expected to save the county $762,301.

The council also approved a recommendation from the Planning Commission to rezone 34 acres of agricultural land in the western part of the city for residential use.

Adapted from a story by Alicia Caldwell, *St. Petersburg* (Fla.) *Times*. Reprinted with permission

20-6. School board meeting

This exercise can be fun for students if you choose five students to play the part of the school board members and read the information as if it were a play. Choose actors from students who are good note-takers and might not need as much practice as the rest of the class. Then let those students write from the script, but ask the rest of the class to write from their notes. The key issue is censorship, and most students will get that in the lead. This story can have a hard-news or impact lead. The rest of the story should contain quotes and discussion of the issue. At the end students can use a list form to itemize the other issues the board discussed. Here are some examples of leads from students' stories.

Kurt Vonnegut, J.D. Salinger and Mark Twain came under fire at last night's school board meeting.

The exchange was prompted by the head librarian's request of funds to update the school's library. Phyllis Laird asked that the district order approximately 200 books, but some of the titles concerned board members.

The Lawrence School Board will consider censoring several books from the school's library.

A heated discussion erupted last night among members of the Lawrence School board over a suggested list of books for libraries in the district's public schools.

20-7. Style quiz corrections

The corrections are in boldface type.

1. The board voted three to two **(3-2)** to have a public hearing about banning some books from the library.

2. The Lawrence city commission **(City Commission)** will discuss an ordinance to bann **(ban)** nudity from bars or restaurants that serve alchohol **(alcohol)**.

3. Mike Wildgen, City Manager, **(city manager)** said the proposed law would only effect **(affect)** busineses **(businesses)** that serve liquor.

4. The first amendment **(First Amendment)** to the constitution **(Constitution)** guaranties **(guarantees)** the right to freedom of expression so the proposed ordinence **(ordinance)** can not **(cannot)** be applied to places that don't serve alcohol, said the county's Chief **(chief)** deputy counselor.

5. Vice mayor **(Mayor)** Charles Shorter was so impressed by the pig that he said he might consider getting one himself.

6. The issue of banning pigs was discussed by the St. Petersburg city council **(City Council)**.

7. One woman brought her potbellied pig to city hall **(City Hall)** when the council debated the ordinence **(ordinance)**.

8. Earvin Magic Johnson had a garanteed **(guaranteed)** contract for $3,100,000 dollars **($3.1 million)**.

9. Burl Osborne is very concerned about preserving the Constitutional **(constitutional)** guarantees of free speech.

10. Osborne said that many colleges had adopted speech codes in the 1990's. **(1990s - no apostrophe)**.

Government
and Statistical Stories

21

Goals

- To teach students how to understand and write budget stories
- To teach students how to write about statistics
- To teach students to use online resources for government and statistics
- To teach or reinforce these style concepts: mills, percents, months without dates, legislature, spelling, money, mph.

Teaching Suggestions

Graphics are especially important to stories with statistics or complicated concepts. Before students write their stories, ask them to use graphics as a tool to help them organize their stories or decide what information should go in a chart and what should go in the body of the story. You can ask them to write a facts or highlights box for some of the main points of a story or a chart for a story that contains many statistics. Governmental online resources abound, and students should be encouraged to check for information in their own communities. You can tailor many of these exercises to your own community by substituting statistics you can find on the Web if you have access to the Internet. Link to them on the Web site for this book: *http://info.wadsworth.com/rich.*

Textbook Exercises

1. Figure your taxes

The figures in this quiz are purposely easy. You may add to this by changing the figures or asking students to do the same thing with several different assessment and tax rates. Here are the answers to the quiz.

1. **a.** $11,500
   b1. $11,500
   b2. $11.50
   b3. $125
   b4. $1,437.50
   c. 15%
   d. 10%

2. Dream home

I usually put students in groups of three and let them plan a home they might buy while they are in college or plan a dream home for their future. They have a lot of fun adding all sorts of amenities, such as saunas, swimming pools, tennis courts and so on – until they figure out the taxes on their mansions.

3. Statistics: Vegetarians beware

Encourage students to use a catchy lead on this story. The point is that some of the worst offenders for fat were the vegetarian sandwich and the tuna salad sandwich, along with the Reuben and grilled cheese sandwiches. The lowest in fat was the turkey sandwich with mustard. Here's the lead on this story from the *San Jose Mercury News:*

> The people who warned us about killer Kung Pao chicken, pudge-producing popcorn and tortilla terror have a new target: the all-American sandwich.
>
> Sandwiches, they say, are piled high with artery-clogging fat.
>
> And not just the Reuben and the greasy grilled cheese sandwich, which ranked first and second for dripping with saturated fat, according to a study released Tuesday by the Center for Science in the Public Interest.
>
> Among the worst offenders were the vegetarian sandwich and the classic tuna. In fact, a tuna salad sandwich has so much fat you might as well eat 80 potato chips instead.
>
> Brigid Schulte, *San Jose Mercury News*

142

4. U.S. Census online research

This exercise is intended to familiarize students with the data that is available from the U.S. Census Bureau. By itself, it does not offer great fodder for storytelling. Students can click into the data for their counties and then explore data for other counties in the state or other states for comparative purposes. A later exercise in the workbook offers more details for communities. If students then click on A-Z and go to P for population projections, they can find more interesting statistics for their states. They could interview experts in the university about social and economic problems related to some of these statistics or they can write a brief story on projected population growth or decline by clicking into the U.S. Census site and searching for population projections: *http://www.census.gov/*

5. Campus budget follow

This assignment is intended for homework if you want to give students practice in research and interviewing for a follow story. Many dire predictions about budget cuts are always made around budget adoption time, so students could check individual departments to see how they coped.

6. Interactive quiz

This is a simple self-graded online quiz that tests students on their knowledge of budget terms. You can give this quiz by printing it out if you prefer. The answers are:

1. b
2. b
3. b
4. c
5. c
6. a
7. b
8. c
9. b
10. b

Workbook Exercises

21-1. Government and weather terms test

Here are the answers:
1. c
2. b
3. c
4. a, b, and c.
5. b and c
6. b
7. b
8. b
9. b
10. a

21-2. Statistics – crime rates

This exercise will give students practice in analyzing data. It is the type of story most reporters have to do at one time or another. Here are some leads from students' papers. Although the statistics are from Colorado, you could apply them to your state.

> Every 30 minutes someone becomes a victim of a violent crime in Colorado, according to statistics released yesterday by the Colorado Bureau of Investigation.
>
> The rate of violent crimes increased an average of 2.5 percent from last year, according to the report. Altogether, that means that over 203,000 violent crimes were committed this year.
>
> "The increase in violent crime reflects a greater social problem than can be solved by police alone," said Mike Stiers, division chief of the CBI. "We are losing the battle here."

21-3. Weather statistics

This exercise also emphasizes analysis of statistics. It should be a very brief story. Here is the original story:

Beginning of dry season is all wet in South Florida

South Florida's weather in November suffered an identity crisis.

Three times during the month, heavy rainfalls doused South Florida – something more typical of October.

Normally, South Florida is lucky to get 3 inches of rain in November, which is supposed to be the start of the dry season.

But this November was the second wettest month in Palm Beach County and the third wettest in Broward and Dade.

More rain fell in Palm Beach County during November – 11.4 inches – than in August.

Broward County's 6.91 inches of November rain was nearly 2 1/2 times the normal amount. And Dade County's 6.41 inches was more than twice the month's 2.84 average.

Where did it all come from? Three times during November, moisture-laden weather fronts stalled over South Florida, a phenomenon more typical of October, said meteorologist Geoff Shaughnessy of the South Florida Water Management District.

[The story ends with a forecast, which you should include in weather stories. This is about cold weather, not rain as in your notes.]

A cold front left this batch of frigid air, but just about the time the weather would normally heat back up, a second cold front is due in, said National Weather Service meteorologist Shawn O'Neil. That means the cold is here through at least Thursday and maybe Friday, he said.

Seth Borenstein, *Sun-Sentinel,* (Fort Lauderdale, Fla.) Reprinted with permission

21-4. City budget story

This is a very difficult exercise that requires explanation of mills and budget analysis. The textbook and this exercise contain tips to help students interpret mill levies. Although it will require use of statistics, urge students to think of the impact on readers. The proposed budget includes a very slight increase in taxes and only a few key points. If you wish, you can ask students to analyze the material, ask questions, and you can make up some quotes to add more interest to the story. Even without additional comments, however, the exercise should help students learn how to analyze a city budget. The main point to stress in the lead is that the impact on taxpayers is minimal. Taxes will remain almost the same, although the city will spend more money on services. Here is an impact lead and a complete version of this story:

Lawrence residents will not see a big increase in their city tax bills in (use number for the next year). Although the city will be spending more, taxes will increase only by 10 cents.

City Manager Michael A. Thrifty presented a $36.6 million budget to the City Commission yesterday, calling for a $2.3 million increase in spending from the current year but no significant tax increase.

City Manager Michael A. Thrifty proposed the (use next year) budget yesterday with only a minimal property tax increase.

Thrifty said that although the city will spend $36.6 million, a 6.6 percent increase from the current year, no significant tax increase is necessary because new construction in the city has increased the tax base to generate more income from property taxes.

Taxpayers will pay $42.20 for every $1,000 of assessed value on their property, a 10 cent increase over the current rate of $42.10. For example, the owner of a house $100,000 house assessed at the city's 15 percent tax valuation rate would pay $633. *[If you used the word "mills," you need to explain that a mill is equal to $1 for every $1,000 of assessed value of property.]*

Some new expenditures in the proposed budget include a 3 percent raise for city employees, additional sanitation workers, a new recreation center and improvement of the downtown business area.

The growing population has generated more garbage, Thrifty said. Two years ago the city collected 34 tons of garbage and this year the rate is up to 44 tons. Thrifty is recommending the addition of six employees for the Sanitation Department.

Water and sewage costs – estimated at $10.9 million – also increased about 6 percent from the current budget and represent about 30 percent of the total city spending. Other key items proposed in the budget include:

- A new 1 percent tax to improve the downtown business district. Thrifty is also recommending that two of the downtown parking lots be repaved with asphalt this summer at a cost of $25,000.
- Approximately $3.2 for police services and $2.3 million for the fire department, together comprising about 15 percent of the budget. No additional personnel are planned.

A major chunk of the budget, about 12 percent, will go to pay off bonds at a cost of $4.3 million to the city. Some of that money will be used to build a new recreation center, approved by voters in the last election with a bond issue.

Property taxes are the major single source of income for the city. For the coming year the city expects to receive about $21 million from property taxes. That includes an additional $5.1 million expected because of the new construction. Other sources include taxes on gas, alcohol, hotels guest tax, and separate taxes for water, sewer and sanitation.

The school district and the county have not yet determined their budgets for the coming year. The combined tax rate this year for the city, school and county was $127 for every $1,000 of property value.

City commissioners will study the budget and conduct public hearings later this month.

21-5. Online statistical profile of a community

Although this is similar to the Census Bureau exercise, this CACI marketing site offers instant access to specific community data. As described in the exercise, if students combine this statistical research with interviews of each other or people in the community, they can gain experience in weaving human interest and statistical material together. This exercise also is designed to make students think critically about statistically information and how it can be used.

21-6. Caffeine consumption

This exercise will give students a chance to write creative leads, interview other students or people about a subject that most people are interested in, and combine research with feature writing. If the caffeine report is no longer available, undoubtedly the Center will have another alarming report. Students should view this site critically and understand the bias of the Center. They can also interview health experts on campus to get balance.

21-7. Style quiz corrections

Corrections are in boldface.

1. The tax rate of 42 mills means residents will pay $42 for every $100 **($1,000)** that their property is assessed.
2. Crime rose 2 and a half % **(2.5 percent)** and robberies increased 21.6 percent.
3. Broward County's 6.91 in. **(inches)** of Nov. **(November)** rain was more than 2 **(two)** times the normal amount.
4. A 12 member **(12-member)** commitee **(committee)** headed by the City Manager **(city manager)** reccomended **(recommended)** that the tax rate be kept at it's **(its)** current level.
5. Taxpayers will pay $42.20 for every $1000 **($1,000)** of asessed **(assessed)** value on there **(their)** property.
6. The budget was recommended by city manager **(City Manager)** Michael A. Thrifty.
7. A mill is equal to $100 **($1)** for every one thousand dollars **($1,000)** of assessed property value.
8. The university is coping with a $6.100,000 million dollar **($6.1 million)** shortfall.
9. The weather forcast **(forecast)** calls for more rain in Palm Beach county. **(County)** and winds up to 30 miles per hour.
10. The bill being debated by the Colorado house judiciary committee House **(Judiciary Committee)** is similar to ones proposed in Legislatures **(legislatures)** in other states.

Crime and Punishment

22

Goals

- To teach the basic elements of crime stories
- To teach students how to read crime reports
- To teach basic court terms
- To teach students how to write a continuing police/court story
- To familiarize students with online resources for crimeStyle concepts: hyphens for joining modifiers, dimensions, addresses, money, fractions, .22-caliber, time, degrees, dates, judgment spelling.

This chapter gives students practice writing crime and court stories. Emphasize that students must be careful to attribute all accusatory information. The stories are geared to a variety of writing techniques, but students should exercise good judgment before writing a soft lead or using a lighthearted tone. Many campus and community police departments now post crime statistics online. Although they are sometime a bit dated, it's a good resource for students. The federal government also has a host of good crime data, and court resources abound. The Web offers students chances to view legal briefs and court opinions, which provide excellent writing opportunities. Check the Web site for this book for direct links: *http://info.wadsworth.com/rich.*

Teaching Suggestions

You may want to review the use of delayed identification leads and reinforce the concepts of libel. Because reporters get so much information about crime stories by telephone, you might present some of the workbook exercises orally instead of letting students write from these exercises in workbooks. Then they can check their accuracy against the material in the workbooks. However, they should work from copies of the police reports and court records so they can learn how to interpret these forms. Although students may write stories from these exercises, encourage them to seek additional information from police and all parties involved when they write actual crime and court stories.

Select the exercises you think your students need or will enjoy the most. I made the mistake of having my students do them all so I could test them, and it was too tedious for them. You might also want to use some of the police and fire exercises earlier in the semester and save the court stories for later.

Textbook Exercises

1. Crime story

This is a standard form for Kansas police departments and may differ in other states. Explain that the basic information is the same, however. You may need to explain military time. Supplemental sheets on police reports contain more information but reporters may not be allowed to see them, depending on the department. Students may write a basic hard-news lead or a more creative one for this exercise. Use a current date.

The most interesting fact in this story is the theft of the bird, a cursing cockatoo. Other than that, the burglary was rather routine. Here are a few leads from students' stories:

> A stolen cockatoo may have a few choice words to say. The bird was stolen last night from a 30-year-old Lawrence man's house, police said.
> The 10-year-old white bird, which answers to the name of Homer, has a limited vocabulary of his name and a few curse words.
> The burglary of the bird and other items from the home of John Smith, 2345 Felony Lane, was reported to police yesterday at 10:56 p.m. by his neighbor, James Doe, who was watching Smith's house while the owner was away.

> A foul-mouthed fowl was among items stolen yesterday from the home of Jon Smith at 1234 Felony Lane.
> Police report that sometime between 7 a.m. and 10:30 p.m., someone broke into Smith's Lawrence residence and took a VCR, a handgun and a 10-year-old cockatoo that responded to the name Homer and had a vocabulary of "damn," "rotten" and a few other curse words. The bird was valued at $1,500 and the total value of the items stolen was placed at $2,050.
> [Story continues with details of the burglary.]

2. Fire story

This exercise can be written in a lighthearted tone because the dog who started the fire lived. It should test students' storytelling abilities. The story also lends itself to pyramid form, leaving the cause to the end if students give some foreshadowing and hold the reader's interest. The original story was written with a hard-news lead.

Hungry pet starts kitchen fire

FORT LAUDERDALE – Tito, a 2 1/2-year-old cocker spaniel, somehow turned on a kitchen stove Saturday, started a major fire and nearly got cooked.

"The dog is a little mischievous," owner Mark Alan Leszczynski said. "I've caught him doing this before."

Leszczynski and a houseguest went to a bar just before midnight on Friday, leaving Tito alone in a ground-floor apartment in the 2700 block of Northeast 30th Place. Apparently searching for food, the dog jumped up on the stove, using one of the knobs for a foothold, and managed to turn the setting to medium-high.

"He has a never-ending appetite," Leszczynski said. "I had just reprimanded him for going into my house guest's suitcase and getting some candy."

Fire officials said some cookbooks and towels on the stove ignited. Soon the kitchen was blazing.

By the time four fire engines and 16 firefighters arrived about 1:15 a.m., Tito had crawled to the front door and, as far as rescue workers were concerned, had died.

"The dog was clinically dead; it had no pulse and no respiration," Fire Battalion Chief Stephen McInerny said.

Firefighter Bill Mock found Tito and took him outside, where paramedics administered cardiopulmonary resuscitation and oxygen. The dog came back to life and was taken to the Animal Hospital of Fort Lauderdale.

"When they brought him to me, he was absolutely in shock and very disoriented," veterinarian Dorian Colorado said. "He and I spent a very long night. He was treated for smoke inhalation."

On Saturday, Tito was in stable but guarded condition. But the blaze killed four gray finches, caused more than $9,000 worth of damage and left Leszczynski temporarily homeless.

Leszczynski said he was happy just to have Tito alive. "He was my biggest concern. I'm a big-time animal lover and an advocate of animal rights."

Fire officials said it is not uncommon for pets to be caught in house fires. They said it is unusual to revive them from the dead.

"That's twice in a little more than a year we've revived dogs that have been clinically dead as a result of a fire," McInerny said. "We're getting pretty good at it."

Ken Kaye, *Sun-Sentinel* (Fort Lauderdale, Fla). Reprinted with permission.

3. Court terms

Most students know the story of Goldilocks and the Three Bears, and this test gives them a chance to be creative. One foreign student who never heard the childhood story wrote about Gold E. Locks, a locksmith. If you have many international students, you might have to explain the original story or let them make up anything. Students usually enjoy this. Check for spelling and context.

4. Court hearing

You can assign students to cover a local court hearing if that is feasible. You might also tape a segment from Court TV and use that in class, or you can use find court documents on the Web. Access Findlaw and search for court decisions in your state: *www.findlaw.com* or link to it from the book's Web site for chapter 22.

5. Civil court case

This exercise was based on a fun story in a Fort Lauderdale newspaper. You might ask students to check their own courthouses for name change petitions. The original story focused on three petitions, but this exercise is slightly easier. The point of the exercise is to make students interpret a court record and write a conversational story.

Workbook Exercises

22-1a–b. Police reports

These records of a motor vehicle accident and a burglary will give students practice reading the reports. Ask students to decide if a description of the suspect in exercise 2B is necessary (it is not) and when it might be. In the past descriptions of the suspect(s) were often a standard part of the story, but several newspapers are questioning using racial identifiers. In this case, although the suspect is white, does that make a difference?

22a. Motor Vehicle Accident

This is just a basic news story that should feature a delayed-identification lead. Change the age to correspond with the current year.

> A 33-year-old (your town) woman was injured yesterday in a two-car collision yesterday at the intersection of 13th and Missouri streets.
>
> Brenda M. Doolittle of the 1200 block of Pennsylvania Ave. [use exact address if that is your newspaper's style] was treated for bruises and released [call the hospital] from Memorial Hospital.
>
> Police said Doolittle was traveling east on 13th Street when her Ford Escort was struck by a Honda sedan driven by Scott Collier, give age, of the 1200 block of Green Street.
>
> Doolittle was cited for not wearing a seatbelt and Collier was cited for failing to yield the right of way.

22b. Burglary

This is also a standard hard-news story, but the interesting point is that the suspect said he was seeking food and shelter.

> A homeless man broke into the Salvation Army building last night in search of food and shelter, police said.
>
> Joseph Stanton is being held in the Shawnee County jail on charges of attempted burglary and criminal damage to property.
>
> Police said they responded to an alarm at the Salvation Army at 515 SE Mission at 1 a.m. and caught a man running from the building.
>
> "I was trying to find some food and I had no place to stay," police said Stanton told them.
>
> Police said a window was broken but there was no indication if any food was taken.

22-2. Burglary

This exercise will reinforce the hourglass technique explained in Chapter 12. It is a useful technique for police reporting.

Student's version:
They got caught with their hands in the proverbial cookie jar.
Five juveniles, ages 11, 14 and 15, were charged with breaking into a food supply truck with a crowbar and stealing assorted boxes of candy, cookies and snacks worth more than $500.

Original story:

5 charged in snacks theft

HOLIDAY, Fla. – Five Holiday youths have been charged with breaking into a food supply truck with a crowbar and making off with assorted boxes of candy.

More than $500 worth of treats was taken from the truck, including a case of Milky Way candy bars, three cases of M&Ms, boxes of cheese crackers and popcorn and a carton of chocolate creme-filled cookies, Pasco Sheriff's Office spokesman Jon Powers said.

The names of the five boys – an 11-year-old, a 14-year-old and three 15-year-olds – were withheld because they are juveniles. They all were charged Tuesday with burglary to a vehicle, and they all admitted to the crime.

Powers said the stealing started late Monday or early Tuesday when two of the boys, who are brothers, saw a Lance Inc. food truck in a parking lot on Darlington Road. Lance supplies food for vending machines.

According to Powers and reports from the Sheriff's Office, the older brother, 15, took a crowbar from a neighbor's yard and pried the padlock off the truck's rear door.

He and his brother, 11, then allegedly took a carton of candy from the truck. They later told the other boys about what they had done, Powers said.

The boys tried to carry the goodies home but the boxes became too heavy for them, Powers said. They left a 50-pound box of Milky Ways on a bench in front of a Winn Dixie supermarket, according to reports.

St. Petersburg (Fla.) *Times.* Reprinted with permission.

22-3. Fire fatality

This story can be written with a basic hard-news lead or a softer lead focusing on the rescue attempts. Students should get the fatality high in the story, either in the lead or the first few paragraphs. Here is one example of a soft lead from a student's version followed by the original story, which features a hard-news lead and hourglass form.

Student's version:

Darren Nitz said he didn't think much about the fire above his apartment Monday morning until he heard that two neighbor boys were trapped in their apartment.

Nitz said he put one of the boys, 14-year-old Michael Fuson, on his back and carried him outside. Nitz and another neighbor, Brad Lindsey, were unable to reach the boy's brother who was trapped in his bedroom. Ten-year-old Kenneth Fuson died in the fire.

Michael Fuson is in critical condition at Emanuel Hospital and Health Center's burn unit with second- and third-degree burns over a third of his body.

Boy dies in fire; brother rescued

A 10-year-old boy died and his older brother was burned over a third of his body Monday when a searing fire swept through their Southeast Portland apartment, where they'd apparently been left alone.

A neighbor was able to pull Michael Fuson, 14, from the apartment at 15758 S.E. Division St. but was unable to reach 10-year-old Kenneth A. J. Fuson in his bedroom.

Michael Fuson was in critical condition at Emanuel Hospital and Health Center's burn unit with second- and third-degree burns on his hands, arms, face, neck, back, buttocks and thighs. He was breathing with the help of a ventilator.

The children's mother, Linda Lee Fuson, arrived at the 32-unit apartment complex after the firefighters, who were on the scene at 6:39 a.m., said Neil Heesacker, a spokesman for the Portland Fire Bureau. Officials did not know Monday morning where she had been.

Firefighters sifted through the rubble looking for a cause of the blaze that was hot enough to burn through the floor, blister the gypsum board walls and melt the family's television set. Three pet birds also died.

A fire investigator credited a neighbor, Darren Nitz, 31, with saving Michael Fuson's life. Nitz lives on the first floor of the Anderson Villa apartments; the Fuson's home was one floor above.

About 6:35 a.m. Nitz heard neighbors pounding on his door and yelling about the fire. He didn't think much about it at first, Nitz said, until someone said two children were trapped in the apartment. Michael was about seven feet from his bedroom door, lying as though he'd been crawling toward the front door.

"He was saying, 'I can't, I can't' and rolling over and over," Nitz said. "I said, 'We've got to get out of here.'"

Nitz tried to grab hold of the youth's arm but couldn't because he was so badly burned. So Nitz put the youth over his shoulder and carried him outside. Michael told his rescuer that Kenneth still was upstairs.

Nitz went back to the top of the stairs, but the flames had reached the front door. Another neighbor, Brad Lindsey, 24, grabbed a fire extinguisher at the bottom of the stairs and followed on Nitz' heels.

"It was fully going when we got up there," Lindsey said. "Just after we got up there, it just vacuumed and shot right across" the stairway.

Lindsey and Nitz retreated back down the stairs.

"There was no way either of us could do anything about it," Lindsey said.

Firefighters brought the fire under control at 7:04 a.m., 15 minutes after a second-alarm sent additional firefighters and equipment.

The blaze caused an estimated $50,0000 damage to the building and $10,000 damage to the apartment contents. Fire officials estimated the value of the building at $480,000 and the family's belongings at $80,000.

The fire also caused smoke damage to the apartment of Pat and Lisa Hampton, who live across the stairs from Linda Fuson. Lisa Hampton is Fuson's sister.

Heesacker said fire in an enclosed area such as an apartment can push temperatures to 1,700 degrees Fahrenheit near the ceiling and 1,000 degrees on the floor.

Holley Gilbert, *The Oregonian*. Reprinted with permission.

22-4. Court terms quiz

Here are the answers:

1. b
2. b
3. c
4. b
5. a
6. b
7. c
8. b
9. c
10. b
11. b
12. b
13. a
14. b
15. c

22-5. Mummy saga

This exercise has always been fun for my students at first. Then they get tired by the fourth part they write because they have to keep including background. And that's the point of the exercise. I prefer to conduct the press conferences myself and let students ask questions. Acting as sheriff, I either make up answers or follow the basic information that is included in the workbook. The other major point of the exercise is to make sure they don't write that a woman was arrested on charges of failure to report a corpse as the lead for the first day. Although you should caution students not to be too silly with their leads, they should get the concept of the mummy in the lead or the idea that the woman tended her husband's corpse for eight years. Another point to discuss is the use of delayed identification at first. Because Carl and Carol have the same last name, suggest that students use their first names or Mr. and Mrs. to differentiate them. The style will vary according to different newspapers, so either could be correct. By the third day they might consider using the woman's name in the lead. Here are a few examples of leads:

Day One:

> Carol Truelove had been caring for her husband, Carl, for the last eight years. She changed his clothes daily and took time to talk to him every day. There was only one problem: Carl Truelove had died eight years ago.
>
> Carol Truelove, 48, pleaded guilty yesterday to the charge of intentionally failing to notify a coroner promptly of a death. She had been arrested (day of the week), after police found her husband's body in a mummified state in a rear bedroom of her home, according to court records.

> Or in a hard-news version:

> A rural Knoxville woman was arrested today when sheriff's deputies found a mummified corpse, believed to be her husband, in her home.
>
> In the second or third graphs get details about the corpse and the woman's name. Back it up with information about the houseguest.

Day Two:

> A rural Knoxville woman who cared for her husband's corpse in her home for eight years pleaded guilty today to failing to report a death. Her houseguest for a year, a dentist from Chicago, also pleaded guilty to the same charge.
>
> Knox County Sheriff Mark Shoemaker said the corpse had been reduced to leathery skin and bones. . .

Day Two - next step: When students have just about finished writing their story, I stop them and say, "New developments." Then I conduct a press conference and ask them to rewrite the top of the story. Judge how much time you have in class and interrupt them when you think they will have enough time to rewrite the story. The first part isn't as important as the lesson of changing the top of a breaking news story. Here's a sample lead:

> "A woman who pleaded guilty to concealing her husband's death by keeping her corpse in her home for eight years, faces new charges of forging his signature on a document to gain access to his bank account."

Day Three: This part of the exercise should test students' ability to include new information and background without taking the reader for granted. Stress that readers may not have seen earlier stories. You can make this lesson very brief because by now students will begin to tire of the story.

22-6. Campus crime statistics

The statistics on this Security on Campus site *www.campussafety.org* are usually a few years old, but the exercise is worth doing because journalists often have to write crime statistics stories. This exercise also offers students a chance to see how much information related to their communities is available online. The all-crime Web site *www.apbonline.com* also offers students a chance to see how crime makes fascinating news and can serve as models for writing crime stories. That site has had financial difficulties and may no longer be online, but I've listed it here just in case it remains because the information is great.

22-7. Court cases

This exercise gives students a chance to view court records without digging through files at a courthouse. You can preview court cases and choose one that you think might be of interest. Try to select one that has good detail so they can write stories that are rich in detail and have human interest.

22-8. Style quiz corrections

1. John Powers, a spokesman for the Pasco Sherrif's **(Sheriff's Department)**, said the boys left a 50 pound **(50-pound)** box of milky ways **(Milky Ways)** on a bench.

2. The robber was described as a black man in his middle 20's **(20s)** about five ft., 10 in. and 140 lbs. **(5 feet, 10 inches and 140 pounds)**.

3. The fire in the apartment at the 2,700 **(2700)** block of Northeast 30th Pl. **(Place)** caused an estimated 9000 dollars **($9,000)** worth of damage.

4. The boy suffered second and third degree **(second- and third-degree)** burns over 1/3 **(one third)** of his body.

5. The weapon was a 22-caliber **(.22-caliber)** handgun.

6. Firemen **(Firefighters)** arrived on the scene about six thirty in the morning **(6:30 a.m.)**

7. Fire in an apartment can reach 1,700 ° **(1,700 degrees)** near the ceiling.

8. The defendent **(defendant)** was sentenced to five years' **(years)** in prison.

9. The mummified body was found on January 30 **(Jan. 30.)**

10. The plaintiff prays for judgement in excess of ten thousand dollars. **(The plaintiff is seeking judgment (no e) in excess of $10,000.)**

Disasters, Weather and Tragedy

23

Goals

- To teach students how to write complex disaster stories
- To teach students how to write human-interest sidebars
- To familiarize students with online resources for disaster and weather
- To teach students how to report and write about grief

Teaching Suggestions

This chapter is geared to advanced students or beginning students toward the end of the semester because the information is complex and the writing skills required involve both hard-news and soft-news techniques. If you plan to use the plane crash exercise, try to schedule this lesson so it does not come immediately before the winter or spring break when many students will be traveling by air.

This version of the textbook and workbook was written shortly after the World Trade Center tragedy, which most students will remember and many may have been affected personally. You can use that tragedy as an example or others to discuss the importance of sensitivity and reporting the human elements.

When you are teaching disaster coverage, discuss how information changes rapidly, especially death tolls, and how reporters must be prepared to cope with chaos. Reinforce how they must be prepared – taking change for telephone calls to the newspaper or cellular phones, finding alternative routes to the scene of the tragedy and gathering information for graphics as well as a story.

This chapter also lends itself to a discussion of ethics. Some ethical concerns can be: What is the reporter's role in helping victims of tragedy? How can reporters be sensitive when interviewing grieving people? Why do the media publish stories about individuals involved in tragedy?

This chapter also attempts to teach students how to ask sensitive questions when they are interviewing people involved in a tragedy. I ask students to get in small groups – usually three to four students – and list all their fears about interviewing grieving people. Then we discuss the concerns of each group and group and reporting techniques that address those fears – from taking tissues to terminating an interview.

Although weather is not always related to disaster stories, natural disasters require knowledge of weather terms and sources. For that reason, I have included weather in this chapter. You might assign some basic weather features before teaching the section on natural disasters. Encourage students to check out the online resources on the Web site for this book at *http://info.wadsworth.com/rich.*

Textbook Exercises

1. Disaster coverage

This is a basic brainstorming exercise that may be helpful, especially if you ask students to include visual tools, such as empowerment boxes, facts boxes, maps and other graphics for which they would have to gather information. You can also ask students to list the sources they would contact and where they would go first in the event of a disaster.

2. First day airplane crash story (Day 2 is in the workbook)

This exercise is designed to teach students how to organize massive amounts of information and how to use material from the chart for perspective – such as whether this is the worst crash in a decade or the second-worst and so on. It is best used on deadline but will take students about an hour or 90 minutes to write the first part and an hour to write the Day 2 exercise (in the workbook).

The role-playing technique, asking students to imagine if they were waiting for relatives or loved ones on that plane, also is useful prior to assigning the writing exercise. Ask them what information they would want to know. Then help students use this information to draft a hard-news lead, which should include the death toll and other crucial information. For this story, I stress that the lead may be longer than leads for many other stories students have written, because it must include so many elements that readers need to know immediately.

Ask students to read all the notes in the exercise and to draft a plan before they begin writing this story. You also could ask students to write a highlights box as an organizing tool or as a graphic accompaniment to the story. If you wish to tailor this exercise to your own area, ask students to use the name of the nearest metropolitan airport in your area; you could even ask them to find out the names of the sources.

For ease of grading and to save time, I use the checklist that follows to see if students have included the material I think is important. You can either use it to check the stories yourself or have students evaluate themselves. You also might ask students to write a sidebar using some of the human-interest quotes. The chart of major plane crashes is only for perspective purposes. You may add more recent crashes if you want students to check the almanac.

Before or after students write the exercise, you can discuss whether vivid description – such as body parts – should be included in the story and how gory the details should be. Many students are tempted to leave out all description of the scene, a problem that can generate good class discussion.

The lead on the first-day story should include an estimated death toll, name of the airline, where it crashed, where it was from, when it crashed and possibly that it crashed in a thunderstorm. The organization of the rest of the story is more flexible. Students should evaluate whether information from P.R. Informer about the safety record and renovation of the airport belong in the story (It is too promotional). If they have checked the chart, they will find that this is the worst plane crash death toll in a decade in the United States. That factor should be high in the story, either in the lead or first few graphs. The almanac lists three crashes in other parts of the world with higher death tolls.

Here are leads from students' stories:

A Delta Airlines jetliner, Flight 313 from Dallas, crashed yesterday at Kansas City International Airport while attempting to land during a heavy thunderstorm, killing at least 200 people.

A Delta Airlines jetliner carrying 275 passengers crashed on the edge of a runway at Kansas City International Airport yesterday during a violent thunderstorm. Authorities fear that at least 200 people are dead in what may be the worst airline crash of the decade in the United States.

Here is a more complete version:

In the worst U.S. air disaster in the past 10 years, a Delta Airlines passenger jet en route from Dallas crashed and burst into flames Wednesday at approximately 3 p.m. at Kansas City International Airport, killing at least 200 people.

Flight 313, carrying 275 passengers and nine crew members, was due to land at 2:30 p.m. in Kansas City. Twenty-five people seated in the rear of the L-1011 jetliner survived, but the pilot, co-pilot and flight engineer were confirmed dead. The fate of several passengers and crew members is unknown.

Many of the passengers originated from Kennedy International Airport in New York and boarded the flight in Dallas for the final destination to Kansas City.

John L. Smoke, fire marshal for KCI, said the nose of the plane apparently exploded on impact just at the edge of the runway in the C concourse. The tail section broke away from the rest of the plane and remained intact, resting just 150 feet from the edge of the runway, which was covered with a sea of foam. Charred metal, suitcases, and body parts were strewn over about 500 feet.

Scores of plastic yellow blankets covering the dead lined the area. Survivors lying on stretchers were moaning and screams filled the air.

"I have never seen so much terror in people's eyes," said Samuel L. Savior, an ambulance driver on the scene. "It's horrifying."

No official cause has been determined, but Retired Coast Guard Adm. Patrick Bursely, a member of the National Transportation Safety Board, said weather factors such as wind shears are suspected because of the violent thunderstorms that struck Kansas City shortly before the plane crashed.

Wind shears, which are sudden and violent changes in wind direction, were responsible for several other plane crashes. Winds were as high as 65 mph in some parts of the city.

"I heard this earsplitting crackle. I think it was lightning," said Milton I. Goldberg, a survivor from New York who was on his way to visit his daughter in Lawrence. "I looked out the window and saw the wing crack. The next thing I heard was a deafening explosion. From that point on, all I heard was screaming. The cabin began to fill with smoke. . . . It was terrifying."

He said one of the flight attendants grabbed him and threw him out the emergency door. "I'm lucky to be alive," he said.

P. R. Informer, information director for KCI, said it appeared that weather was a factor in the crash. "It was a freak accident," she said. "We safely land and depart planes all the time in thunderstorms, and this one did not seem prohibitive to air traffic," she said.

Informer said a passenger list would not be released until the families of the dead and injured are notified.

[Story can continue with information about hospitals, morgue, more comments from eye-witnesses, and other people.]

Airplane Crash Checklist – Day One

Here is a list of the information that should be included in the first-day story. The information is not listed in the order for the story, although the first 12 items should be in the first few paragraphs of your story.

Information	Good	Fair	Omitted
Death toll	_____	_____	_____
Name of airline	_____	_____	_____
Location of crash	_____	_____	_____
Origination point	_____	_____	_____
Flight number	_____	_____	_____
Time of crash	_____	_____	_____
Number of survivors	_____	_____	_____
Number of passengers	_____	_____	_____
Type of plane	_____	_____	_____
Destination (if different from crash site)	_____	_____	_____
Weather	_____	_____	_____
Suspected cause	_____	_____	_____
Crash description	_____	_____	_____
Description of scene	_____	_____	_____
Fate of pilots and crew	_____	_____	_____
Perspective (high in story if crash one of worst)	_____	_____	_____
Eyewitness accounts	_____	_____	_____
Survivors' accounts	_____	_____	_____
Human interest quotes	_____	_____	_____
Hospitals	_____	_____	_____
NTSB investigation	_____	_____	_____
Temporary morgue	_____	_____	_____
Airport closed	_____	_____	_____

Workbook Exercises

23-1. Plane crash – Day 2 story

Day 2 of the exercise is designed to test whether students can identify the strongest news element for a lead – that the current weather forecast was not conveyed to pilots. The rising death toll also can be the second-day lead. Make sure students have included a recap of the basic information of when and where the crash occurred. Here is an example of a student's story:

The pilot of Delta Flight 313, which crashed at Kansas City International Airport during a severe thunderstorm......[give day] and killed 234 people, may not have received an up-to-date weather forecast, investigators said yesterday.

"There is indication of a weather forecast being delivered to controllers some 10 minutes before the crash, and that was not passed along to the pilot," said retired Coast Guard Adm. Patrick Bursely, the lead investigator for the National Transportation Safety Board.

He said investigators had recovered the black box which contained recordings of the pilot's last communications.

"It appears that both controllers involved and the pilots involved in this accident were not concerned about the weather," he said.

The death toll from the crash rose yesterday to 234 and 50 people survived, making this the worst domestic airline crash in the past 10 years.

A thunderstorm containing lightning and winds between 60 and 65 mph arose over the airport about 30 minutes before the crash.

Bursely said it appears the plane might have hit a wind shear – an upward air current surrounding a center of downward winds that can force a plane to plummet.

The Lockheed L-1011 was en route from Dallas when it crashed Monday at 2:55 p.m. About 215 of the dead have been identified so far.

[Continue with news from medical examiner and quotes from survivors.]

23-2. Explosion mainbar

This exercise is designed to make students organize a lot of material on deadline. The exercise also contains an ethical problem. One of the sources, a council aide, gives the name of a woman who says her relatives are in the house that exploded. He gives the names of the relatives, who are not confirmed dead. Students should evaluate whether his comments should be included in the story, because if the people have died, it is unlikely that their relatives would have been informed of the fact by officials. Here is the original story:

Gas line explodes; 2 die
Duffy St. homes ablaze

A gasoline pipeline exploded this morning, sending flames 100 feet into the air, killing at least two people and injuring several more residents in the same San Bernardino neighborhood decimated by a train derailment almost two weeks ago.

The explosion occurred at 8:11 a.m. from a 14-inch pipeline from Calnev gas company. The pipeline, which carries unleaded fuel from Colton to Nevada, is buried six feet underground.

Seven homes were ablaze.

David Andries of Calnev said the pipeline ruptured and sprayed fuel on the houses.

"We don't know the cause of the break. It could have been the train, obviously," Andries said.

The dead were found inside a home on Duffy Street. One body was burned beyond recognition. The other victim was believed to be a man, said Paul Allaire, a San Bernardino Fire Department spokesman. Firefighters were still looking for a third victim in the home.

The ruptured pipeline is buried six feet beneath the ground near where a Southern Pacific freight train derailed and crashed into a string of houses on May 12, killing two crew members and two boys in a home.

Councilwoman Valerie Pope-Ludlam, who was at the scene Thursday morning described it this way:

"A woman ran out of her house, she left behind her sister, her cousin and a 6-month-old baby inside, and she looked back and the house blew up behind her," Pope-Ludlam said.

Miretta Brumlow, who lives at 2351 Adams St. near the site was at the first aid center set up at Macy Street. Brumlow was still wearing a nightgown.

"I felt my whole house shake. I thought it was an earthquake. Then I looked out and I saw the fire and I just started crying," Brumlow said. "I ran to the bedroom and got my daughter and grandson out, then I started looking for my pets and then I just had to get out.

"I think my cats are still in there. Everything I own was in that house," said Brumlow, who is a student at San Bernardino Valley College but hasn't attended since the railroad disaster because she's been afraid to leave her children at home.

"Thank God I didn't go to my class at eight o' clock this morning," she said.

Bill Stewart, an insurance agent, was visiting a client, Martha Franklin in a house in the 2300 block of Donald Street.

"We were sitting at the table and we heard this loud noise and it just started getting bigger. I ran to the window and looked out and could see nothing but smoke; then we both hit the floor," Stewart said.

"We waited for it to blow over, but it didn't go away. Then we started to head for the door and when she opened the door, the smoke just started rolling in. We looked outside the grass was burning – green grass burning. Everything was burning, even the concrete," he said.

The thick cloud of gray-black smoke from the explosion was reported visible from as far away as Riverside and Ontario. Highland Avenue at Macy was closed to motorists as fire officials and Calnev officials began to try to put the fire out.

Southern California Gas Co. workers were in the neighborhood to shut off the gas lines to avoid any possibility of natural gas explosion.

San Bernardino City Attorney Jim Penman, who toured the area from a helicopter, said, "We were assured by the pipeline people it was safe and the experts who examined it said there was no danger."

The seven burn victims, whose names were not available, were taken to San Bernardino County Medical Center, where their conditions were not available late Thursday morning, officials said.

At the medical center, officials said Tina Blackburn was in serious condition with second- and third-degree burns over 15 percent of her body. Michael Howard had burns on his hands, his wife, Janet Howard, had received third-degree burns and their two children, Shirley, 1, and LaKedra, 2, were being treated for smoke inhalation.

Resident Diane Tucker was treated for minor cuts.

The Red Cross had set up an evacuation center at the Job Corps Center, 3753 Kerry St., where by 10 a.m. 30 residents from Duffy and Donald streets neighborhoods had already arrived, said Theresa Schorder of the Red Cross. Two vans and a bus were being used for the evacuation.

Calnev officials said the pipeline can carry more than 3.3 million gallons of fuel – jet fuel, gasoline and diesel – which flows through the 14-inch pipeline daily. The pipeline was carrying unleaded gasoline.

Pipeline General Manager Jed Robinson said valves along the pipe fall into place whenever anything in the pipe starts to flow backward, toward Colton where the pipeline starts.

However, a valve near the fire may not be completely closed, he said, and that could influence the time it takes to put out the fire.

"With that kind of a volatile fuel, you have to use some sort of foam," Robinson said. "Normally where there is not an awful lot of fuel, you just contain it and try to burn out."

He said he did not know how much fuel is in the pipe.

Joe Gutierrez and Carl Yetzer, *The* (San Bernardino, Calif.) *Sun.* Reprinted with permission.

23-3. Explosion sidebar

This exercise is relatively simple and is intended only to help students deal with human-interest material. Stress that students should mention some background about the explosion even if the information will be in an accompanying mainbar because the sidebar should be self-contained. Here is the original:

Anger smolders on Duffy Street

Beneath the shock and the tears lies the anger.

It smoldered in Patrick Thomas' eyes as he sat holding his 15-month-old daughter, Lisa, in a Red Cross evacuation shelter set up at the Job Corps Center on Kerry Street.

Thomas was among the refugees from the neighborhood where a gas pipeline exploded Thursday morning, sending balls of fire racing through their homes.

Like other residents living near the side of the May 12 train derailment on Duffy Street, he thought the worst was over.

His home at 2313 Adams St. survived the train wreck unscathed. But when he last saw the rented house Thursday, flames were crawling up one side. It was situated five houses from another Adams Street house that blew up.

"I am mad," he said. "I am mad as hell – at the railroad, at whoever put that fuel line in, at whoever built those houses over a fuel line, at the city for not doing something."

Other residents focused their anger on the company that operates the pipeline, Calnev Pipeline Co.

"It makes me sick that this fire happened – especially if somebody knew it needed to be repaired. Somebody ought to be hung out to dry," said Mark Kingston.

Another Duffy Street resident's fury knew no bounds.

"They had no damn business trying to patch no pipe up anyway," said Vincent Hemphill. "They should have discontinued that until they fixed it."

Hemphill, 25, grew up in the house at 2604 Duffy St. Even if his home survived, he said he won't go back.

No one should return to those unlucky streets, he said.

"It's messed up. I think they should just, like, take the whole neighborhood and move us out of there. It's a disaster for all of us now," he said.

Maxie Charles of 2441 San Benito Court said the federal government should step in and provide emergency relief.

"This should be declared a disaster area. And if they want to keep these pipelines, they should pay us off and we will be happy to move out," he said.

Many of the residents believe they were betrayed.

"If it wasn't safe for us to live, why'd they tell us it's OK to move back there?" wondered Georgia Mitchell.

Mitchell's house was destroyed and her daughter, a son-in-law and two grandchildren were injured.

Just two weeks ago, Mitchell watched the train derail in front of her home at 2337 Duffy St.

Jan Carrera said she counted on Calnev officials to be correct when they announced the pipeline was sound after the train crash and that it was safe to return to the neighborhood.

"We believed them that they had it under control," she said.

The right side of Clemmie Williams' face still stung where a medic had smeared white salve over a burn.

Williams, 51, said two days ago he whiffed something in the air near his San Benito Court home that smelled like a mixture of fuel and ammonia.

The odor lasted about 10 minutes, and Williams let it pass without concern.

"They said there was no leakage so we assumed it was OK."

Bonita Campbell walked around the nightgown, robe and slippers she wore when the explosion occurred.

Her family got out of their San Carlo Avenue home safely; her two dogs waited in her car.

"Right now I don't know what to think. I don't know what to do. I know I can't continue to live like this not knowing what's going to happen."

Theresa Walker and Carla Wheeler, *The* (San Bernardino, Calif.)*Sun.* Reprinted with permission.

23-4. Coping sidebar

Choose a type of disaster that your community might experience: floods, tornadoes, hurricanes or earthquakes. Using the online resources linked to the Web site for this book, ask students to research the topic and write a sidebar about tips for coping. They also could interview disaster relief experts in their communities for additional information.

23-5. Basic weather feature

If you are having a hot, cold, dry, wet or other unusual stretch of weather, assign students to write a weather feature. Or send them out to interview people if it's just an unusually nice day. Begin the assignment by brainstorming various angles they might take. For example, how are businesses affected if it is very cold or hot. Are fans or heaters sold out? How much is the university spending on snow removal or grounds maintenance if the weather is unusual. Make sure they get some human-interest angles.

Add a research component by having students check the Internet for records in this month and include a forecast. They could also compare their community to others. You'll find this information in links for the book or *www.weather.com*. Other sites with weather for specific cities include CNN and USA Today.

23-6. Covering grief

As mentioned in the beginning of this chapter, I brainstorm with students about their fears of interviewing grieving people, and we discuss solutions. To further their understanding of grief, students can link to the grief resources for this chapter on the book Web site and read some of the personal essays or advice. They can write a feature based on some of the Internet personal essays or interview each other about some loss in their lives. For example, many students have lost parents or grandparents, a friend or a pet. The online resources include several resources for dealing with the loss of a pet. Or you could ask them to write questions that they would ask if they had to interview one of the people who have experienced great loss.

Profiles

24

Goals

- To teach students how to report and write personality profiles
- To teach students selectivity for vignettes
- To teach students to use visual tools, such as facts boxes

Teaching Suggestions

This chapter combines many of the feature techniques, such as storytelling, use of anecdotes and descriptive writing. Caution students to gather concrete details and to use show-in-action description rather than adjectives to describe their profile subjects.

Although some workbook exercises are offered in this chapter for writing practice, the best way to teach this chapter is to assign students to gather their own material for a profile.

Students often will choose a source they think is interesting but who may lack a newsworthy focus. You need to remind students that even personality profiles need a nut graph explaining why they are writing about this person.

Class project: One semester when my students were especially weak in reporting, I tried a class project as an alternative to individual profile assignments. A student at our university had disappeared, and after three months, police still had no clues. Our project was to do an in-depth profile of this student by getting the points of view of friends, family, childhood experiences and so on. The project involved investigative reporting techniques, record searches and techniques of interviewing grieving friends and relatives who were convinced that he had died. The theory of police and friends was that the student had jumped into the river one night after he had been drinking and that he had drowned, but there was no proof of that. (Several years have passed and his body still has not been found.) Each student was assigned a different portion of the profile.

We brainstormed questions in class and discussed problems and progress. The students had to type up their notes, and I duplicated them for the rest of the class. When it was time to compile the profile, the students had to use all the notes and write individual versions of the profile. I believe this group approach helped students realize how thorough they could be and how to write an in-depth profile.

The class-project approach can be used for in-depth profiles of politicians or other people in your community, but the subject needs to be sufficiently complex for this to work. Although less preferable, you might assign students to work in pairs or teams on a profile.

The Web site of The Academy of Achievement Web offers excellent question/answer interviews of some famous people. The interviews can serve as a good class writing exercise. Check the Web site for this chapter in the book at *http://info.wadsworth.com/rich.*

Textbook Exercises

1. Newsworthy person

For many years I had assigned students to find profile subjects on campus, particularly professors who were involved in some interesting research or who were teaching a new course. But with scores of journalism students from many classes seeking profile subjects, this assignment can be a burden for the professors, who may not be able to spare the time, and for students who may face unwilling subjects. In the past few years I have asked students to find profile subjects in the community instead of on campus because they are more likely to be writing about community people for a local newspaper.

Review students' profile budgets before they decide upon a subject. Students often want to write about some disabled student as though the person is exceptional just for his or her disability. Or students will say they know an interesting person such as a graduate teaching assistant, but the subject really lacks a newsworthy focus.

2. Vignettes

The vignettes need some frame to make sense. One year my class did people behind the scenes on campus. Another year we used the frame of multiculturalism, and students wrote vignettes about people from various cultural, racial and ethnic backgrounds. If you are teaching during a semester when community or student senate elections are scheduled, you might assign vignettes of candidates. You could also choose an issue frame, such as Julie Sullivan's model of people living in a run-down area of your town, social service workers in your community or even portraits of night people who work at hospitals, all-night restaurants or other jobs throughout the night.

3. Celebrity profile

Students may have difficulty gaining interviews with the top athletes on campus or other celebrities. However, there may be some value in asking them to do research and find unusual questions they would ask.

As an alternative to a profile, consider assigning students to ask an athlete on campus who is frequently interviewed what kinds of interview questions he or she likes and doesn't like. Students can ask what bores the athlete in an interview, what keeps him or her interested and recommendations the person has for reporters. Or you could invite a celebrity to class to address these questions, and ask the students to write a profile based on their questions.

4. Coaching

Pair up students as in the coaching activities suggested in previous chapters. Ask them to define the focus of their profile and then coach each other by asking some of the questions in the text and other questions that come to mind. This is particularly helpful at varying stages of the profile process -- before and especially after reporting.

5. Slice-of-life snapshots

This exercise is similar to the vignettes except you can get the class to brainstorm a theme or frame of reference for the short profiles. Students may enjoy doing snapshots of night people, because many students stay up so late and haunt the night places themselves. In our town, a few all-night restaurants are good sources for these vignettes. People who work at night also make good profile subjects. Encourage students to show these people in action in their work, play or study. Urge students to use observation and get specific details.

Workbook Exercises

The best way to teach profile writing is to have students interview a subject. These exercises can reinforce some techniques in class.

24-1. Autobiographical profile

This exercise is intended to help students focus on events and descriptive details. It is easier for them to write about themselves if they do it in third person. Guide them to choose only details that relevant when they write the profile. If they have trouble beginning the free-writing part of the exercise, you could give them some key words to get started, such as: fear, tired, excited. An alternative is to have them write about a close friend or relative. Also, encourage them to include anecdotes. Discuss how they can transfer this type of thinking to profiles of other sources. This exercise also works in conjunction with the Chapter 26, Media Jobs and Internships. It helps students choose crucial information about themselves that they might include in a cover letter or use in a job interview.

24-2. Web autobiography

This also works as a precursor to the resume-writing chapter. For the Web, writing should be much shorter. A popular design is a one-screen introduction, which will limit students to less than 25 lines of type. Although they can often create a one-screen home page and have another page with more information about themselves, this exercise will help them condense their thoughts and consider how writing for the Web should differ from print presentation.

24-3. Background research for profile

You could alter this by asking students to do research on a well-known leader in your community or in the university. An easier way to do this in class is to have students click into the celebrity databases linked to the book's Web site and write a profile based on that information. You can also use the online information as a way to ask students to devise interesting questions they might ask if they had to interview any of the celebrities they chose. You can decide which celebrities you want students to research or let them choose their own.

24-4. Slice-of-life profile

This exercise is difficult because the interview is relatively dull. But it is indicative of many basic community profiles students might have to do. In fact, you could ask them how they would have made the interview better and what kinds of questions they might have asked. It will give students practice in organizing material. Here is the published version:

Mail delivery's her bag

Letter carrier Nancy Workman was concerned when one of her patrons failed to pick up his mail for several days.

"He wasn't someone who consistently picked up his mail every day, but his mail just kept piling up, and after a while, it worried me," Workman said.

Workman didn't want to overreact. But then she noticed the front door of his house. His screen door was covered with flies. Workman went next door and asked the man's neighbors to call the police. Upon arrival, the police discovered that the middle-aged man had died of a heart attack several days ago.

"I was hoping I was wrong, but I had a really eerie feeling about the whole situation," Workman said. "It was really scary because I knew this man, and suddenly he was dead."

Workman, who has worked as a letter carrier for five and a half years, said discovering a dead patron is by far the most bizarre experience she has had during her employment with the United States Postal Service.

"Most of my job is fairly routine," she said. "Each day, I put the mail for my route in proper delivery sequence, and then I walk my route, delivering the mail."

Workman has a walking route that covers approximately 23 square blocks. She spends between four and four and a half hours each day delivering the mail.

"I come in each morning at 7:15 a.m., and I sort the mail for about three hours," she said. "Then I deliver the mail, and after that, I work at the office, preparing for the next day until 3:15 p.m."

Letter carriers choose their own delivery routes based on seniority. Workman said she chose her route because it was a flat walking route.

"Most letter carriers prefer driving routes, but driving just never appealed to me," she said. "Walking is tremendous medicine, as it's a great time for reflection."

Workman estimates that she walks almost 12 miles each day. Consequently, she closely monitors weather forecasts.

"Once you're out there, you have no shelter. There's no place you can hide," she said. "The worst thing is sitting at home, worrying the night before a major storm. I have problems sleeping on those nights, just thinking about the coming storm."

She said winter was the most difficult time to deliver the mail, not only because of the weather, but because she encounters fewer people to talk to.

"I love meeting the people on my route and getting to know them," Workman said.

Encounters with dogs are a minor job hazard. Workman carries "dog mace" in her dusty blue mailbag that she totes each day. "I've only had a dog bite me once, and it was very minor, more like a mosquito bite," Workman said. "Dog poop, though, can really ruin your day."

Workman said the benefits outweigh any job hazards.

"I love the outdoors, and I love the freedom of the street," she said.

Workman decided to become a letter carrier in 1986 after talking with a friend who worked for the post office. She took a postal test, and her name was placed on a roster. She was hired in 1988 as a letter carrier.

"This is really a great job for someone with only a high school education," she said.

Workman said she enjoys the unpredictability

"Each day I come in, and I have no idea how much mail there will be," Workman said. "Some days catalogs are the enemy."

But Workman plans to remain a letter carrier indefinitely.

"I really do love this job," she said. "I plan to keep delivering the mail until I can't walk anymore. "

Colleen McCain, *Lawrence Journal-World.*
Reprinted with permission.

24-5. Rosa Parks and/or Charles Kuralt profile

The Academy of Achievement Web site contains very brief profiles and great question-answer interviews. I chose the interviews with Rosa Parks and Charles Kuralt especially because the latter was quite thorough and Kuralt was a media achiever, but you can select others if you prefer. I think this offers students a good class writing experience. You might discuss what other questions they would have wanted to ask.

Access the Web site from the chapter for this book or directly from *www.achievement.org*. Then go to gallery of achievers frames version, so you'll have to click on a category of interest (public service) to locate Rosa Parks and Charles Kuralt. Other interviews students might enjoy are for athletes such as Julius Erving or Coach Mike Krzyzerwski "Coach K" of the Duke Blue Devils. If you wish, students can supplement the information by searching other Web sites.

Computer-assisted Journalism

25

Goals

- To introduce students to simple data base calculations with spreadsheets

Teaching Suggestions

Although this chapter comes near the end of the book and may be taught at any time during the semester, I have begun teaching part of it near the beginning of the semester so my students can use the Internet in researching stories. Each year more students know how to browse, so the first part of this chapter may soon be unnecessary.

I don't use the database material with beginning students unless I have time near the end of the semester. This chapter is not fun to read but it is fun to do, so encourage students to interact with the information. Because of constant changes in technology, some of this information may change and programs you use may be different, so you will have to adjust accordingly. For online resources, check the Web site for this book at *http://info.wadsworth.com/rich.*

Textbook Exercises

1. Occupations spreadsheet

Here is the spreadsheet with the increases and decreases in the number and percentage of occupational changes.

Occupation	Employment 1998	Employment 2008	Change number	Change Percent
Computer engineers	299	622	323	108
Computer support specialists	429	869	439	102
Systems analysts	617	1,194	577	94
Database administrators	87	155	67	77
Desktop publishing specialists	26	44	19	73
Paralegals and legal assistants	136	220	84	62
Personal care and home health aides	746	1,179	433	58
Medical assistants	252	398	146	58
Social and human service assistants	268	410	141	53
Physician assistants	66	98	32	48
Totals	2926	5189		

1. Hate crimes spreadsheet

You can link to the FBI site from Fedstats or directly at *www.fbi.gov*. Then instruct students to explore the Uniform Crime Reports, which list hate crimes. Try to get the most recent statistics. Supplement this exercise by asking students to check their own campus or community police departments and statistics to compare the hate crime figures or other crimes if you prefer.

Here is the full spreadsheet with calculations:

Participating States	Incidents Reported 1995	Incidents Reported 1999	Number change	Percent Change
California	1,751	2,295	544	31%
New Jersey	768	663	-105	-14%
New York	845	602	-243	-29%
Massachusetts	333	492	159	48%
Michigan	405	492	87	21%
Texas	326	335	9	3%
Arizona	220	307	87	40%
Florida	164	303	139	85%
Washington	266	300	34	13%
Illinois	146	297	151	103%
Ohio	267	283	16	6%
Minnesota	285	266	-19	-7%
Maryland	353	252	-101	-29%
Pennsylvania	282	244	-38	-13%
Virginia	51	238	187	367%

Connecticut	87	212	125	144%
Colorado	149	189	40	27%
Tennessee	25	149	124	496%
Oregon	152	135	-17	-11%
Indiana	35	127	92	263%
Missouri	135	119	-16	-12%
Kentucky	81	100	19	23%
Utah	107	74	-33	-31%
Wisconsin	45	73	28	62%
South Carolina	26	61	35	135%
Oklahoma	37	51	14	38%
Idaho	114	49	-65	-57%
Rhode Island	46	44	-2	-4%
Delaware	45	42	-3	-7%
Georgia	49	40	-9	-18%
Nevada	68	40	-28	-41%
North Carolina	52	37	-15	-29%
Montana	11	34	23	209%
Iowa	29	33	4	14%
Maine	75	23	-52	-69%
Vermont	10	23	13	130%
New Hampshire	24	21	-3	-13%
New Mexico	24	19	-5	-21%
South Dakota	5	14	9	180%
Arkansas	7	9	2	29%
Louisiana	7	7	0	0%
Alaska	8	6	-2	-25%
District of Columbia	4	6	2	50%
Mississippi	6	2	-4	-67%
North Dakota	3	2	-1	-33%
Wyoming	19	2	-17	-89%
Totals	7,901	9,112	1,211	15%

3. Population growth

This exercise is also intended to introduce students to the wealth of information available on the U.S. Census site. You can link to the statistics from the book Web site. To find the statistics within the U.S. Census site, start with the home page *www.census.gov,* go to Subjects A-Z to P for population. Then click on estimates, to Place and County Subdivision Population Estimates to Annual Time Series of Population Estimates to find your own state. You could also have students work with other statistics, comparing their states to others instead of using the county population growth estimates. The point is to teach them to import statistics into Excel and sort figures.

Workbook Exercises

25-1 Sort and calculate #1

This exercise takes students through the steps of sorting and calculating, so it is self-explanatory. When students copy the figures, make sure they save frequently while typing them. If you are using a program other than Excel, adjust the instructions accordingly. Here are the answers in the various sorting forms the students should get.

a. Media jobs that pay the most:

Art directors	56,880
Public relations managers	54,540
Writers and authors	42,270
Public relations specialists	39,580
Editors	39,370
Graphic designers	34,570
Broadcast technicians	26,950
Photographers	22,300
Announcers	19,800

Sort #2 : Graphic designers will have the largest increase in numbers (190)
Sort #3: Occupation with the greatest change: public relations managers (36.3%)

These figures show the number and percent changes.

Occupation	Total		2000-2010		Median annual
	employment		change		earnings
	(000's)		in total		(Dollars)
			employment		
	2000	2010	Number	Percent	
			(000's)		
Graphic designers	190	241	51	26.7	34,570
Public relations specialists	137	186	49	36.1	39,580
Photographers	131	153	22	17	22,300
Writers and authors	126	162	36	28.4	42,270
Editors	122	149	27	22.6	39,370
Public relations managers	74	101	27	36.3	54,540
Announcers	71	68	-4	-5.5	19,800
Art directors	47	56	10	21.1	56,880
Broadcast technicians	36	40	4	10.2	26,950
Film and video editors	16	20	4	25.8	34,160

25-2. Sort and calculate #2

Most campus newspapers carry at least one story about sexually transmitted diseases. The statistics on chlamydia are from the Centers for Disease Control databases. This exercise involves the same techniques but gives students more practice in doing the calculations. The directions are the same as in the previous exercise.

You can add to this exercise by having students access the CDC site and read reports about sexually transmitted diseases and write a story to go with their statistics. Use the Web site for the book or link directly to the CDC at *www.cdc.gov*. Here is how the final statistics should look.

Total calculations

age group	male	female	difference	%difference
10-14	451	8,717	8,266	95%
15-19	19,298	139,256	119,958	86
20-24	25,439	104,929	79,490	76
25-29	12,625	38,553	25,928	67
30-34	6,326	14,733	8,407	57
35-39	3,280	6,441	3,161	49
40-44	1,537	2,659	1,122	42
45-54	1,124	1,536	412	27
55-64	271	876	610	70
65+	266	291	20	7
totals	70,617	317,991	247,374	

Age group with highest percentage = 10 to 14 year olds

10-14	451	8,717	8,266	95%
15-19	19,298	139,256	119,958	86
20-24	25,439	104,929	79,490	76
55-64	271	876	610	70
25-29	12,625	38,553	25,928	67
30-34	6,326	14,733	8,407	57
35-39	3,280	6,441	3,161	49
40-44	1,537	2,659	1,122	42
45-54	1,124	1,536	412	27
65+	266	291	20	7
totals	70,617	317,991	247,374	

Age group with highest numbers of males = 20 to 24 year olds.

age group	male	female	difference	%difference
20-24	25,439	104,929	79,490	76
15-19	19,298	139,256	119,958	86
25-29	12,625	38,553	25,928	67
30-34	6,326	14,733	8,407	57
35-39	3,280	6,441	3,161	49
40-44	1,537	2,659	1,122	42
45-54	1,124	1,536	412	27
10-14	451	8,717	8,266	95%
55-64	271	876	610	70
65+	266	291	20	7

Age group with highest numbers of females = 15-19 year olds.

age group	male	female	difference	%difference
15-19	19,298	139,256	119,958	86
20-24	25,439	104,929	79,490	76
25-29	12,625	38,553	25,928	67
30-34	6,326	14,733	8,407	57
10-14	451	8,717	8,266	95%
35-39	3,280	6,441	3,161	49
40-44	1,537	2,659	1,122	42
45-54	1,124	1,536	412	27
55-64	271	876	610	70
65+	266	291	20	7
totals	70,617	317,991	247,374	

25-3. Write a story from statistics

The press release will help students get started, but they should analyze the data and add more information to make a story. Suggest that they analyze whether men make more than women, whites more than people of color and which age groups make the most money with higher degrees.

25-4. Analyze data: Unmarried couples

Students can see that the South has a higher number of unmarried couples, but why? Suggest that they look further into U.S. Census data to analyze which states have a higher percentage of unwed couples living together. They could also check the Census for additional data about women getting married at a later age and other related data. Stress that analyzing data is just a start for researching a story. Students still need to do additional reporting and find other sources.

Media Jobs and Internships

26

Goals

- To help students apply for jobs and internships
- To help students prepare cover letters and resumes
- To familiarize students with online media job resources

Teaching Suggestions

Ask students to write a cover letter and resume. If you use the portfolio grading method, you can ask them to include the letter and resume when they submit their portfolios to you for an evaluation. Preferably before the end of the semester, ask students to prepare their materials for an internship or job application. If they wait until the end of the semester, it is usually too late to be considered for an internship. In fact, this is a good exercise near the beginning of the semester because it will help you get to know the students. Even if students do not have any idea where they would like to apply for a job or internship, ask them to choose some possibilities for job applications.

Another assignment that might be helpful: Assign students to write a story about the job prospects for graduating students in their fields. Check Web resources for online jobs on the book's Web site:
http://info.wadsworth.com/rich.

Textbook Exercises

1. Interview employers

You can ask students to write a report or a story about the job characteristics employers seek from job applicants in their field of interest. Discuss their findings in class. They might also ask employers to discuss cover letters and resumes they like and don't like to receive.

2. Write about yourself

It is very difficult for students to write cover letters that reveal anything interesting about themselves. If you ask them to write a brief feature about themselves in the third person, it can help them pinpoint some of their unusual or interesting characteristics. As mentioned in a previous chapter, if they write a brief autobiography of less than 25 lines, that could serve as a one-screen Web resume or introduction to a resume.

3. Cover letter and resume

I consider this one of the most important exercises in the course. Students usually have no idea how they can sell themselves in cover letters. Make students revise their cover letters and resumes until they are perfect.

Workbook Exercises

26-1. Research the organization

Encourage students to read the newspaper, magazine or media kit of an organization where they would like to work. That is preferable to using a directory. However, students are not aware of directories that list a variety of organizations, so this exercise can familiarize them with ones in their fields.

26-2. Interview graduates

You may prefer to ask some graduates to come to your class.

26-3- 5. Workbook exercises   - self explanatory

Appendix - Style Tests

Here are corrections for the style tests; each one is worth five points except in quizzes with 25 items, with each one worth four points.

Style Test A-B

1. 10 a.m.
2. all right
3. accommodate
4. among
5. 5
6. affect
7. 2600 Barker Ave.
8. Tudor Road
9. bad
10. alumna
11. bachelor's
12. Alzheimer's disease
13. aide
14. Broad Street
15. 333 Sunset Road
16. 19 years old
17. Ph.D.
18. robbery
19. buses
20. 9-year-old

Style Test C-E

1. cannot
2. has
3. espresso
4. East Coast
5. employee
6. which
7. consensus
8. is
9. Jan. 18.
10. east, two
11. Centers for Disease Control
12. $37.
13. drunken
14. who
15. that
16. e-mail
17. Constitution
18. 33 cents
19. capital
20. dean's list

Style Test F-K

1. misdemeanor
2. Fewer
3. well
4. U.S. Department of Justice
5. harassment
6. House of Representatives
7. Internet
8. Jell-O
9. 5-year-old, kidnapped, kindergarten
10. It's
11. Ku Klux Klan
12. judgment
13. fliers
14. fewer
15. Kidnapping
16. city hall
17. manslaughter
18. children
19. its
20. City Hall

Style Test L-0

1. lay
2. lay
3. legislature
4. like
5. mph
6. $50 billion
7. $20 million
8. were
9. marijuana
10. celebrate
11. occurred
12. five miles
13. was
14. online
15. more than
16. OK
17. No.1
18. Time magazine
19. master's degree
20. No one

Style Test P-S

1. 5 percent
2. Police
Department
3. potatoes
4. 125 pounds
5. 233 Mountain Road
6. innocent," (comma
inside quotes)
7. stationery
8. sheriff
9. Supreme Court
10. were
11. passers-by
12. principle
13. The Rev. John Paul
14. were
15. parentheses
16. 1990s
17. A's
18. privileged
19. "We shall overcome." (period inside
quotes
20. Senate

Style Test T-Z

1. teen-ager
2. who
3. World Wide Web
4. that (with the
understanding that
you need the clause
for clarity of which
building)
5. whose
6. Whom
7. ZIP
8. 35 mph
9. vs.
10. warning
11. Xerox
12. Who's
13. Postal Service
14. they're
15. totaled
16. traveled
17. Web
18. who
19. whom
20. Sen.